AF798537

Enrich your Grammar

A Direct and Practical Approach

8

by

H.S.Bhatia (M.A.)
Ex Sr Lecturer (English)
A. S. College, Khanna (Punjab)

Edited by

Reita Sharma (M.A., B.Ed.)
Ex Teacher
Delhi Public School, Dhanbad

Vimla Kaul (M.A.)
Ex Teacher
Carmel Convent, Dhanbad

Name : ____________________

Class : ____________________

School : ____________________

the Bookmaster

DS Publishers India

Published by
DS Publishers India
7/7 Ansari Road
Daryaganj
New Delhi 110002
INDIA
+91 (11) 4156 3757
info@dspublishers.com
www.dspublishers.com

25th Impression 2025

9788180230141

Typesetting by
Lovika Arts

Cover Design by
White Mice Media

Printed in India at
Balaji Offset

₹330

UNIT 1

ARTICLES (A, AN AND THE)

*The determiners **a**, **an**, and **the** are usually called Articles.*

Articles 'a' and 'an' are Indefinite Articles.
Article 'the' is the Definite Article.

Uses of a / an / the

1. **A**, **an** or **the** can be used before a countable noun which represents a class.

   Examples
   (i) **A** cow gives milk. (All cows give milk.)
   (ii) **The** dog barks. (All dogs bark.)
   (iii) **An** elephant trumpets. (All elephants trumpet.)

2. **A** or **an** is usually used before a countable noun where it stands for one in number.

   Examples
   (i) She bought **an** egg. (one egg)
   (ii) I have **a** cat. (one cat)

3. **The** is used before nouns to particularize them.

   Examples
   (i) Jane bought **a** new *novel*. The novel had a black *cover*. (Particularizing a singular noun)
   (ii) Tony bought five eggs. **The** *eggs* were fresh. (Particularizing the plural noun)

4. **A** or **an** is used with a noun complement.

   Examples
   (i) She is a teacher.
   (ii) He is a doctor.
   (iii) Mr David was an engineer.

5. **A** or **the** is used with few and little.

Examples

(i) There were only **a** few students present in the class.
(ii) Harris has eaten **the** few grapes that were in the basket.
(iii) There was **a** little water in the jug.
(iv) He has lost **the** little money he had in his pocket.

6. **A** is used in exclamations before singular countable nouns.

Examples

(i) What **a** beautiful flower it is!
(ii) What **a** fine day today is!

7. **A** is used before certain numerical expressions.

Examples

a hundred
a dozen
half **a** dozen
a thousand

8. **A** is used before Mr / Mrs / Miss + surname.

Examples

(i) **A** Mr Jack has come to see you.
(ii) **A** Miss Mary wants to talk to you on phone.
(The speaker does not know either Mr Jack or Miss Mary.)

9. **The** is used before the unique objects.

Examples

(i) **The** sky
(ii) **The** sun
(iii) **The** moon
(iv) **The** world
(v) **The** earth
(vi) **The** universe

10. **The** is used before the names of newspapers, magazines, etc.

Examples

(i) **The** Times
(ii) **The** Sun
(iii) **The** London Express
(iii) **The** Blitz

11. **The** is used before the names of holy books.

Examples

(i) **The** Ramayana
(ii) **The** Old Testaments
(iii) **The** New Testament
(iv) **The** Quran
(v) **The** Bible
(vi) **The** Gita

12. **The** is used before the names of trains, ships, aeroplanes, roads, etc.

Examples

(i) **The** Super Fast Express
(ii) **The** Queen Elizabeth
(iii) **The** MIG - 21
(iv) **The** Grand Trunk Road

13. **The** is used before the names of rivers, gulfs, mountain ranges, bays, channels, etc.

Examples

(i) **The** Amazon
(ii) **The** Persian Gulf
(iii) **The** Bay of Bengal
(iv) **The** Indian Ocean
(v) **The** English Channel
(vi) **The** Alps

14. **The** is used before the names of peoples (nations).

Examples

(i) **The** Indians
(ii) **The** French
(iii) **The** Germans
(iv) **The** Muslims
(v) **The** Jews
(v) **The** Christians

15. **The** is used before the names of imaginary lines.

Examples

(i) **The** Longitude
(ii) **The** Latitude
(iii) **The** Equator
(iv) **The** Tropic of Cancer
(v) **The** Tropic of Capricorn
(v) **The** Axis

16. **The** is used as an adverb.

Examples

The more, **the** merrier

17. **The** is used before a superlative degree.

Examples

(i) John is **the** most intelligent boy in our class.
(ii) Dolly is **the** tallest girl in our street.

NOTE : 'A' is used with the words which give a consonant sound e.g., a pen, a one rupee note, etc.

'An' is used with the words which give a vowel sound e.g. an orange, an hour, etc.

Omission of Articles

The Article is omitted:

1. before Common Nouns used in the modest sense.

Examples
(i) **Man** is mortal.
(ii) **Woman** is the mother of mankind.

2. before Proper Nouns.

Examples
(i) **Nina** is my classmate.
(ii) **Ashoka** was a kind king.

> **NOTE : When an article is used before a Proper Noun, it becomes a Common Noun.**
>
> *Examples*
> (i) Monica is **the Madam Curie** of our class.
> (ii) He is **the Einstein** of our class.
> (iii) We need **a Sunil Gavaskar** to win this match.

3. before the names of games.

Examples
(i) She plays both **cricket** and **tennis** well.
(ii) We play **hockey** in the evening.

4. before Material Nouns.

Examples
(i) **Milk** is essential for children to keep good health.
(ii) We get **silk** from a silkworm.

But we may write:
(i) **The milk** of this cow is sweet.
(ii) **The silk** that we imported from China was of good quality.

5. before Abstract Nouns.

Examples
(i) **Love** begets love.
(ii) **Bravery** is the quality of the brave.

NOTE : When an abstract noun is qualified by an adjective, it may take 'the'.

Examples

(i) **The childhood** of Abraham Lincoln was full of misery.
(ii) **The honesty** shown by the little child is commendable.

6. before the names of meals.

Examples

(i) We had **lunch**.
(ii) She had **dinner**.

7. before the names of certain phrases, etc.

Examples

(i) We reached **home** late at night.
(ii) We were caught in **storm**.

8. when a noun is preceded by a possessive determiner.

Examples

(i) She kept **her word**.
(ii) This is **my last attempt** to reach the summit.

Exercise 1

Fill in the blanks with 'a', 'an' or 'the'.

1. My uncle is ________ teacher in ________ university.
2. ________ Himalayas lie in ________ north of India.
3. I have been waiting for you for ________ hour.
4. She is ________ English writer who lives in England.
5. ________ Europeans have florid faces.
6. Kalidas is ________ Shakespeare of India.
7. Mr. Mugabe, ________ honourable man, lives near ________ equator.
8. Who is ________ owner of this house? I think, Mr Jack.
9. Do you know ________ exact time of the start of ________ exhibition?
10. She has ________ headache. So, I'm on my way to call in ________ doctor.

11. Honey usually plays ________ piano but, now he is playing ________ violin.

12. Harry has ________ dog, which always barks at ________ strangers.

13. ________ Rajdhani Express is ________ fastest train in India.

14. Annie bought two kg mangoes. ________ mangoes looked quite good.

15. Jack has bought ________ bicycle. ________ bicycle is green.

Exercise 2

Insert 'a', 'an', or 'the', if necessary; otherwise, place a sign of cross (×).

1. I was reading ________ horror novel when somebody knocked on ________ door.

2. While crossing ________ road I saw ________ egg of a hen lying there.

3. ________ mother loves her child from ________ core of her heart.

4. Where's ________ child? I want to have ________ talk with him.

5. She walked forward, put ________ books on ________ table and turned ________ back to her seat.

6. ________ Ganges is ________ holy river of India. It meanders through ________ zigzag hilly track before entering ________ plains.

7. ________ old man started running after ________ bus but could not catch it.

8. There was ________ collision between ________ lorry and ________ car just round ________ corner of my house.

9. I found ________ coin on ________ road while I was walking leisurely.

10. I've ________ big white and ________ black cat, which looks more like ________ dog.

11. Julie has ________ white and ________ brown dogs. Because of their rough fur, they look ferocious and wild but in ________ reality they are ________ best examples of ________ gentleness.

12. Last night, ________ lightning flashed and ________ sky rumbled every now and then.

UNIT 2

INDEFINITE PRONOUN

The words given in the following box are Indefinite Pronouns.

somebody	anybody	someone
nothing	something	anything
everything	everybody	anyone
no one	nobody	one

Examples

(i) **Something** is better than **nothing**.

(ii) **No one** can face him physically for his being so robust.

(iii) **Somebody** told me that Mr Sam was going to install a sugar factory in Canada.

(iv) Is there **anything** to eat? No, there is **nothing**.

(v) There wasn't **anyone** whom we could ask for an inn in the city.

(vi) **Everybody** was in high spirits in the party.

(vii) **Everything** was going well till the last moment.

(viii) **One** should do one's duty honestly.

Exercise

Fill in the blanks with Indefinite Pronouns such as someone, anyone, everyone, no one, nothing, none, something, somebody, anybody, nobody, etc.

1. Is there ________________ who can see that distant star?

2. ________________ told me that Mr Harris had lost not only his wealth but also his faith.

3. ________________ should try to elevate himself to the status of a reputable man.

4. _______________ can enter these premises without permission.

5. I want _______________ to help me carry this heavy box to my room.

6. Is there _______________ who we may ask for help? No, there isn't _______________.

7. _______________ can be done in such unfavourable circumstances.

8. _______________ likes to be treated unceremoniously.

9. Did _______________ ever expect such uncharitable remarks from such a dignified personality?

10. Is there _______________ important? No, there is _______________ .

11. _______________ should take care of one's old parents.

12. _______________ succeeds like success.

13. Even at present _______________ meaningful can be done.

14. _______________ knows that our earth revolves round the sun.

15. There's _______________ important in this magazine.

16. _______________ should save _______________ from his income for the rainy day.

17. Is there _______________ at home?

18. _______________ came downstairs and opened the door.

19. _______________ asked me for help though I was ready to oblige.

20. _______________ knows the real meaning of life on earth.

UNIT 3

THE ADJECTIVE
Degrees of Comparison

There are three Degrees of Comparison of Adjectives.

1. Positive Degree
2. Comparative Degree
3. Superlative Degree

Positive Degree

This degree shows the amount of a particular quality in a person, thing, place or animal.

Examples

Jack is **fat**.

Comparative Degree

This degree shows the comparison of a particular quality between two nouns or pronouns.

Examples

John is **fatter** than Jack.

Superlative Degree

This degree shows the maximum amount of a particular quality among more than two nouns or pronouns.

Examples

Timmy is the **fattest** among the boys.

The common rules to get Comparative and Superlative Degrees from Positive Degree are given below.

1. The Adjectives of one syllable (one sound) usually take **er** and **est** to make their Comparative and Superlative Degrees respectively.

Positive	Comparative	Superlative
sweet	sweeter	sweetest
warm	warmer	warmest
bright	brighter	brightest
fast	faster	fastest
slow	slower	slowest
cold	colder	coldest

2. The words of one syllable ending in **e**, take **r** and **st** to make their Comparative and Superlative Degrees respectively.

Positive	Comparative	Superlative
able	abler	ablest
fine	finer	finest
brute	bruter	brutest

3. In Adjectives ending in **y**, usually **y** is changed into **i** and then **er** and **est** are added to make their Comparative and Superlative Degrees.

Positive	Comparative	Superlative
busy	busier	busiest
cheeky	cheekier	cheekiest
crunchy	crunchier	crunchiest
easy	easier	easiest
crazy	crazier	craziest
flashy	flashier	flashiest
floppy	floppier	floppiest
funny	funnier	funniest
grubby	grubbier	grubbiest
heavy	heavier	heaviest

4. When the Positive Degree is a word of one syllable ending in a single consonant preceded by a short vowel the consonant is usually doubled before adding **er** and **est** to it.

Positive	Comparative	Superlative
fit	fitter	fittest
big	bigger	biggest
thin	thinner	thinnest
hot	hotter	hottest

5. The Positive Adjectives having more than two syllables or ending in ful, ous, etc. most often take **more** and **most** to form Comparative and Superlative Degrees respectively.

Positive	Comparative	Superlative
careful	more careful	most careful
doubtful	more doubtful	most doubtful
industrious	more industrious	most industrious
luxurious	more luxurious	most luxurious
lustful	more lustful	most lustful
nervous	more nervous	most nervous
loquacious	more loquacious	most loquacious

6. The Degrees of some Adjectives are changed in entirely irregular ways.

Positive	Comparative	Superlative
good/well	better	best
ill/bad/evil	worse	worst
little	less/lesser	least
many/much	more	most
far	farther/further	farthest/furthest
fore	former	foremost/first
nigh	nigher	nighest/next
old	older/elder	oldest/eldest

Note : The word 'fore' is not commonly used now. Similarly 'nigh', 'nigher' and 'nighest' are also not a part of the common usage of words now.

Exercise 1

Correct the following sentences and rewrite them. Place a tick mark if the sentence is already correct.

1. Alex is the most outstandingest student in our class.

____

2. One of my cousins is in the habit of talking non-stop for hours together. I think he is the loquaciousest person in the world.

____

3. Henry takes immense pleasure in hooting and whistling. He is the most noisy student in our class.

____

4. The car Mr Hood bought yesterday is more flashier than yours.

____

5. Maria beat the curd for a few minutes to make it soft and fluffier.

____

6. There are all kinds of comforts in his house. So, it is the most luxuriousest house in the world.

____

____

7. Yesterday, a car met with an accident on the highway. All the occupants got injuries but the condition of the driver was the most worst.

____

____

8. His next plan was even atrocious than the previous one.

____

9. Now, the naughty boys thought that it was time for them to take risk. Tony seemed to be the more audacious among them all.

____

____

10. He was brought up in the most gloomiest place in the world.

____

Interchange of the Degrees of Comparison

Read the following sentences carefully.

1. (a) **Positive** : John is as fat as Gomes.
   (b) **Comparative** : Gomes is not fatter than John.

2. (a) **Comparative** : Tina is taller than any other girl in our class.
   (b) **Positive** : No other girl in our class is so tall as Tina.
   (c) **Superlative** : Tina is the tallest girl in our class.

3. (a) **Superlative** : Shimla is one of the coldest places in India.
   (b) **Comparative** : Shimla is colder than most other places in India.
   (c) **Positive** : Very few places in India are so cold as Shimla.

Exercise 2

Change the Degree of Comparison without changing the meaning.

1. (a) Quinine is more bitter than most other medicines.
   (b) Positive : ______________________
   (c) Comparative : ______________________
2. (a) Lolita is as industrious as Miley.
   (b) Comparative : ______________________
3. (a) The Rajdhani Express is one of the fastest trains in India.
   (b) Positive : ______________________
   (c) Comparative : ______________________
4. (a) He is the most delightful singer in the world.
   (b) Positive : ______________________
   (c) Comparative : ______________________
5. (a) No other place in the world is so horrifying as this one.
   (b) Comparative : ______________________
   (c) Superlative : ______________________
6. (a) This bird has the most iridescent feathers.
   (b) Positive : ______________________
   (c) Comparative : ______________________
7. (a) I have got one of the finest purses in the world.
   (b) Comparative : ______________________
   (c) Positive : ______________________
8. (a) Only a few monuments in the world are as beautiful as the Taj Mahal.
   (b) Comparative : ______________________
   (c) Superlative : ______________________
9. (a) This is one of the longest trains in the world.
   (b) Positive : ______________________
   (c) Comparative : ______________________
10. (a) This is the most expensive hotel in India.
   (b) Positive : ______________________
   (c) Comparative : ______________________

UNIT 4

PAIRS OF ADJECTIVES

Much, Many

Many is used with plural countable nouns. It stands for a large number.
Much is used with uncountable nouns. It stands for a large quantity.

Examples

(i) There weren't **many** birds on the branch of the tree.
(ii) **Many** people were present there to listen to the Prime Minister.
(iii) There wasn't **much** rice left in the bag.
(iv) There was **much** sugar in the box.
(v) I've **much** work on hand.

Note : Much is used as an adverb before an adjective in the comparative or superlative degree.

Examples

(i) She is **much** better today.
(ii) This horse is **much** the best in the stable.

Exercise 1

Fill in the blanks with 'much' or 'many'.

1. ______________ members of the club were absent from the meeting.
2. How ______________ sugar do you want?
3. How ______________ ripe mangoes are there in the basket?
4. There are ______________ pens in the bag.
5. She needs _______ money to buy ______________ exotic dolls.
6. ______________ cattle were grazing down there in the meadow.
7. To make ______________ noise is bad. The names of ______________ students have already been struck off the rolls for this.
8. ______________ girls danced in the party.

9. An apple contains ________________ pips.

10. There was too ________________ noise emerging from the class.

11. ________________ plants have a very thin bark.

12. When there are ________________ students in a class, there will be ________________ noise.

13. We need ________________ rice right now. Should I give you ________________ bags of rice?

14. There were ________________ bowls on the shelf and each bowl contained ________________ sugar.

15. There are ________________ bottles in the cupboard. Each bottle contains ________________ water.

16. A tiger is ________________ bigger than a cat.

17. There is ________________ truth in his statement.

18. She is ________________ the worse for her failure in the examination.

Few, A Few

A few stands for a small number. It has a positive meaning.

Few stands for hardly any. It has a negative meaning.

Examples

(i) Only **a few** boys could understand what their teacher said.
(ii) **A few** of my relatives are earning handsome money.
(iii) **Few** villages in India are provided with modern facilities.
(iv) **Few** persons will believe your strange story.

Little, A Little

A little stands for not much. It is used with uncountable nouns. It has a positive meaning.

Little stands for almost nil quantity. It has a negative meaning.

Examples

(i) There was **a little** water in the jug.
(ii) There was **a little** ink in the inkpot.
(iii) She has **little** hope of success.
(iv) There is only **a little** hope of patient's recovery.

Exercise 2

Tick the correct answer.

1. She has only ________ dresses but all of them are quite attractive. (a few, few)
2. I want to discard this pen. It is of ________ use to me. (little, a little)
3. She has ________ sense of understanding and cannot distinguish between good and bad. (little, a little)
4. ________ persons can show patience in such unfavourable circumstances. (few, a few)
5. There is ________ ink in this inkpot. So, I've to buy a new one. (a little, little)
6. There was only ________ water in the jug. I drank it but it did not quench my thirst. (a little, little)
7. There was ________ to choose from among the ________ gifts available in the small gift shop. (a little, little)
8. There are ________ plants, which do not purify the air. (a few, few)
9. There is only ________ milk in the jug and I think it will not be sufficient for the morning tea. (a little, little)
10. ________ learning is a dangerous thing. (a little, little)
11. I have ________ time for reading such articles. (a little, little)
12. There are ________ people in cold countries who have practical experience of life in the countries near the equator. (a few, few)

The Few, The Little

The few refers to number. It is used when a specifically small number of nouns is shown as disposed of in some way.

The little refers to quantity. It shows the disposal of a small quantity of something.

Examples

(i) **The few** coins the little girl had in her pocket, fell off as she began to skip over the rope.

(ii) **The little** water there was in the pond, has evaporated because of the increased heat of the sun.

Exercise 3

Use 'the few' or 'the little' in the following sentences.

1. __________________ water animals there were in this river, have died due to the inflow of toxic effluents from factories.

2. __________________ hope of relief entertained by the common man after the budget, has been belied because of government's somersault in its financial policy.

3. __________________ speck of cloud that had appeared in the sky in the afternoon, has now disappeared in the evening.

4. __________________ who are honest are ridiculed by the many who are dishonest.

5. After the death of his only son, he has lost __________________ faith he had in God.

6. __________________ I had saved after hard work of years, has been spent overnight on my illness.

7. __________________ waves of water that were rising and falling in the lake, have been levelled down because of the sudden stillness of the air.

8. __________________ roses that had bloomed in my garden, have withered because of unusual dryness of weather.

Less, Fewer

Less is used with uncountable nouns. It refers to quantity.

Fewer is used with countable nouns. It refers to number.

Examples

(i) There are fewer girls present in the class today than there were yesterday.
(ii) Please put less sugar in my tea.

Exercise 4

Fill in the blanks with 'fewer' or 'less'.

1. He has ________________ foes but more friends.

2. There are ________________ stars visible tonight in the sky than they were last night.

3. There is _______________ sugar in the ice-cream. So nobody has liked it.

4. She won no _______________ than $500 in the casino.

5. There are _______________ shirts in your wardrobe than in mine.

6. February has _______________ days than March.

7. There is _______________ money in his drawer than in yours.

8. She refused to accept _______________ money than she had been promised to be paid.

9. This basket contains _______________ oranges than that.

10. There is _______________ cheese in the tray than in the box.

Each, Every, Either, Neither

Each refers to the individual person in a group of two or more when the number is limited and definite.

Every refers to all of a group of more than two persons or objects, taken singly, when the number in the group is indefinite.

Either has two meanings:
(a) both
(b) one of the two

Neither is the negative of **either** and it means neither the one nor the other.

Examples
(i) **Each** party has its own flag.
(ii) **Every** man wishes to be rich.
(iii) He can work with **either** hand (both hands).
(iv) **Either** boy can win the race.
(v) **Neither** country was visited by him.
(vi) **Neither** toy is attractive.

Exercise 5

Tick the correct suitable word for each of the following blanks.

1. _______________ man wishes to live a luxurious life. (each, every)

2. You can take _______________ piece of cheese. (either, neither)

3. _______________ girl in our class was given a prize. (each, every)

4. It rained _______________ day during July last year. (each, every)

5. _______________ boy was allowed to go to the zoo. So, they decided to go to see a movie. (either, neither)

6. On ______________ side of the road there was a bed of flowers. (either, neither)

7. ______________ child in the class was asked to sing which he did merrily. (each, every)

8. It is ten days back when I met him at the airport which ______________ man might have wished to visit due to see its splendour, if for no other purpose. (each, every)

9. She lived in a country, ______________ road of which had a blinding gloss. (each, every)

10. ______________ girl was granted permission to attend the meeting. So, they decided to pay a visit to Switzerland. (either, neither)

11. She is ambidextrous. So, she can write with ______________ hand equally well. (either, neither)

12. Ten girls stood in ______________ row at the function. (each, every)

13. ______________ guess about future can be true. (either, neither)

14. ______________ man needs money to live a good life. (each, every)

15. ______________ student should bear in the mind that an impressive demeanour is a great asset. (each, every)

Some, Any

Some is usually used in affirmative sentences. It is used with countable nouns where it stands for **a few**. It is used with uncountable nouns where it stands for **a little**.

Examples

(i) There are **some** spoons on the shelf.
(ii) There is **some** butter in the tray.

> **NOTE : Sometimes 'some' can also be used with interrogative sentences, e.g. Can you give me 'some' sugar?**

Any is usually used in interrogative or negative sentences. It can also be used with either kind of nouns i.e. countable or uncountable nouns.

Examples

(i) Are there **any** eggs in the tray?
(ii) No, there aren't **any** eggs in the tray.
(iii) Is there **any** cheese on the plate?
(iv) No, there isn't **any** cheese on the plate.

> **NOTE : In an interrogative sentence, 'some' is usually used when positive answer is expected and 'any' is used when negative answer is expected. This method is, however, not arbitrary.**

Exercise 6

Fill in the blanks with 'some' or 'any'.

1. "Is there ________ juice in the can?" "Yes, there is ________ ."
2. "Are there ________ boats in the sea?" "No, there aren't ________ boats in the sea."
3. My cousin has ________ exotic toys that he bought from Singapore.
4. I've ________ milk but I don't have ________ sugar.
5. I must have ________ sugar to make a cake.
6. There isn't ________ butter left in the tray. So, please buy ________ butter for me.
7. There aren't ________ eggs left in the tray. You must buy ________ eggs at once because I want to eat an omelette.
8. Is there ________ rice in the bag? Actually I want to boil ________ rice right now.
9. There is ________ tea in the kettle but there isn't ________ milk in the jug.
10. If you don't have ________ grapes, I'll go to the market and buy ________ grapes for the guests.
11. You can't have ________ sweets today because the shops are closed for ________ reason.
12. Would you like ________ fresh pears or should I buy ________ apples for you?
13. "Give me ________ biscuits to eat." "But there aren't ________ biscuits in the box."
14. "Can you give me ________ milk?" "Sorry, I've only ________ milk at present which I have to give to my ailing mother."
15. Is there ________ ink in the pot? I want ________ ink because I've to write important letters.
16. "Have you got ________ sports magazines?" "No I don't read ________ sports magazines."
17. Are there ________ cake slices left in the box? I want to keep ________ slices for the guests.
18. There aren't now ________ animals living in that jungle, although years ago there were ________ wolves and tigers there.
19. There was ________ noise in the street. But, as I went out to find out the reality, I didn't see ________ boys or girls around.
20. She lent me ________ money. But she told me that she would not lend me ________ money in future.

UNIT 5

THE TENSE

There are three kinds of Tenses :

PRESENT TENSE
PAST TENSE
FUTURE TENSE

Each Tense has the following forms :

1. Indefinite
2. Continuous
3. Perfect
4. Perfect Continuous

The Simple Present (Present Indefinite) Tense

The Simple Present Tense is used:

1. *to express the habitual truth.*
   (i) He always goes for a walk before sunrise.
   (ii) I often take a glass of milk before going to bed.
   (iii) He usually goes to office on bus.
   (iv) She rarely does cooking.
2. *to express something that is always true.*
   (i) The sun sets in the west.
   (ii) A penguin has flap type wings, which help it to swim.
   (iii) The countries lying close to the equator are warm because there the rays of the sun fall directly.
   (iv) Japan has to face the maximum number of earthquakes in the world because of its geographical position.
3. *with subordinating conjunctions e.g. unless, if, until, when, before, etc. to express future action.*
   (i) They won't go to the theatre if it rains.
   (ii) They will return home before the sun sets.
   (iii) You cannot go anywhere until I come back.
   (iv) You cannot shoot any photograph here unless you show me your identity card.

4. *to express future.*
   (i) The Superfast Express arrives at 9 p.m.
   (ii) Danny and Martin come as openers of the match.
   (iii) The British Airways first flight takes off at 1 a.m.

The Present Continuous Tense

The Present Continuous Tense is used:

1. *to express an action in progress at the time of speaking.*
   (i) The workers are painting the doors and windows.
   (ii) My sister is cooking some Italian dishes because we are expecting guests in the evening.
   (iii) She is knitting a sweater for her husband.

2. *to express a future state, etc. with 'going to'.*
   (i) Karina is going to be the most intelligent woman ever born on earth.
   (ii) What else are you going to take along with these pastries?
   (iii) Jack is going to celebrate his 20th birthday next Sunday.

Exercise 1

1. Fill in the blanks with correct tenses of the verbs in the brackets. Use Simple Present or Present Continuous Tense only.

1. She usually ____________ (drink) juice in the party but today she ____________ (drink) iced tea.
2. Jack ____________ (paint) a picture. He usually ____________ (do) it late in the evening.
3. My brother often ____________ (play) the piano in the club. But today he ____________ (play) the violin.
4. What ____________ (do) you here? I ____________ (want) to see my pet, Tommy.
5. John ____________ (go) to make his maiden speech in the theatre tomorrow. I ____________ (hope) he'll make a good job of it.
6. His mother will come back before it ____________ (rain).
7. If you ____________ (love) me and your friends, you must pay a visit to India.
8. My uncle often ____________ (go) to office by car but today he ____________ (go) to office on bus.

> **NOTE : The students should also try to understand the difference between the usages of 'by bus' and 'on bus'.**

9. He usually ____________ (smoke) exotic brands but today he ____________ (smoke) an Indian brand.

10. You won't tell all this to anybody else unless you ____________ (ask) to do so.

11. She often ____________ (speak) French but now she ____________ (speak) English.

12. My brother always ____________ (like) to dress in black but at tomorrow's function he ____________ (go) to wear a white dress.

13. Such kind of snakes ____________ (be) usually lazy but this one ____________ (seem) to be an exception.

14. My sister always ____________ (do) painting very well but in today's competition she ____________ (lose) ground.

15. He generally ____________ (play) an impressive tennis but today he ____________ (play) very badly.

16. You should not leave the place until I ____________ (come) back.

17. We'll go for the show when it ____________ (be) twelve by your watch.

18. She ____________ (try) hard for her survival.

19. If you ____________ (tease) him, he will react violently.

20. She always ____________ (work) from dawn to dusk but right from now she ____________ (go) on leave for a week.

Simple Past Tense

The Simple Past (Past Indefinite) Tense is used:

1. *to express actions or events in the past with the adverb or adverbial phrases e.g. yesterday, ago, last week, in 2012, etc.*
   - (i) She finished dinner one and a half hour ago.
   - (ii) I saw a strange bird yesterday.
   - (iii) He met me in 2012 when he was not in high spirits.
   - (iv) I typed nine letters this morning. (Now morning is over.)

2. *to express habitual truth in the past and also to express certain historical truth.*
   (i) He worked hard all his life.
   (ii) The First battle of Panipat was fought in 1526.
   (iii) Once the earth was a ball of gases.
   (iv) He used to take tea in the evening.

Past Continuous Tense

The Past Continuous Tense is used:

1. *to show an action in progress in past time.*
   (i) He was playing hockey when I reached there.
   (ii) They were singing all the evening on Christmas.
   (iii) When we arrived, they were watching a movie on the T.V.
2. *to express two actions at the same time.*
   (i) Tony was painting while her sister was drawing a picture.
   (ii) Ruby was dancing while her sister was singing.
3. *to express plans in the past with the following expression.*
   (i) They were going to buy a brand new Mercedes.
   (ii) She was planning to fly to America.
   (iii) He was going to be the new boss the following month.

Exercise 2

Fill in the blanks with the correct tense of the verbs in brackets. Use Simple Past or Past Continuous Tense.

1. She ____________ (live) in Russia from 1999 to 2003.
2. I ____________ (visit) the Eiffel Tower thrice between 2007 to 2012.
3. My aunt usually ____________ (wear) sky blue saree but that day in the party she ____________ (wear) a bottle green one.
4. When she ____________ (meet) me on the roadside, she ____________ (carry) a gun.
5. On that piece of land the hot wind often ____________ (blow) at noon and the morning ____________ (be) calm but that day a hot and hard wind ____________ (blow).
6. He ____________ (fly) a kite last Sunday.

7. My brother ___________ (dance) while my sister ___________ (sing) in the party.

8. The beat of the drum ___________ (transport) the audience to some other world.

9. She ___________ (put) the papers on the table, ___________ (move) a few paces backwards and ___________ (fling) the door open.

10. None of us could guess what actually she ___________ (look) for.

11. The sky ___________ (be) clear. But after an hour it ___________ (begin) to rain.

12. When I ___________ (go) to see him, he ___________ (listen to) music and his younger brother too ___________ (be) there.

13. In no way he ___________ (be) ready to accept the deal but as soon as I ___________ (show) him some of the bright features of the project, he immediately ___________ (come) round to my view.

14. Sophia usually ___________ (play) the piano but that night she ___________ (play) the Guitar in the club.

15. She ___________ (want) to share her grief with someone but nobody ___________ (show) any sympathy with her. So, she ___________ (keep) weeping through the night alone.

16. It ___________ (be) hardly nine when the guests ___________ (begin) to pour in the hall and soon there ___________ (leave) no room for any more persons.

17. I ___________ (meet) him years ago. Then he ___________ (be) a baby-faced tough guy.

18. His dismal performance ___________ (cause) a long set-back to his reputation but after a few years he ___________ (regain) the title and ___________ (look) satisfied.

19. When I ___________ (see) him he ___________ (talk) to himself about his own rejection by the world.

20. She ___________ (turn) about and ___________ (start) walking ahead while her hands ___________ (brush) her sides.

The Present Perfect Tense

The Present Perfect Tense is used:

1. *in completion of a work in the present time.*
   (i) She has finished her homework.
   (ii) He has just finished his office work.
   (iii) She has not finished cooking, yet.
   (iv) He has already eaten two slices of the cake.

2. *with some of the adverbs e.g. recently, ever, now, before, when, etc.*
   (i) She hasn't ever visited New Zealand, the place famous for kiwis.
   (ii) He has polished not only his own shoes but also those of his wife.
   (iii) Have you heard from your son this week?
   (iv) Our company has recently launched a new range of nail polishes with the slogan "for the women, who care for glamour."
   (v) I always go for a walk when I have got up before 6 am.
   (vi) But I go for breakfast only after I have taken my bath.
   (vii) I've never written such a letter before.

3. *when there is Future Tense in the main clause.*
   (i) We'll play as soon as I've finished my homework.
   (ii) We'll go to see a movie when I've completed painting.

4. *with 'since' and 'for'*
   (i) She has been here since 8 o' clock.
   (ii) He has been the manager of the hotel since 1987.
   (iii) She has lived in the house for five years.
   (iv) Mrs Albert has been in this asylum for three years.

Exercise 3

Fill in the blanks with Simple Past or Present Perfect Tense of the verbs given in the brackets.

1. ____________ you ever ____________ (be) to Australia?
2. Yesterday, a bus ____________ (skid) into a tree.
3. She was brushing down her fur coat when I ____________ (go) to see her.
4. Peter ____________ just ____________ (come) in the office. He'll be going out soon.

5. Our company ___________ (decide) to cut down the prices of its goods. So, in future you'll get our company's products at cheaper rates.

6. We'll go to see your uncle, when I ___________ (finish) frying cheese.

7. I ___________ (not see) him since we ___________ (meet) three years ago.

8. You should never go to bed before you ___________ (have) your dinner.

9. He ___________ (work) in the bank for two years.

10. I ___________ (watch) many a good movie last year. For this year I ___________ (decide) not to waste time any more on movies.

11. Our company ___________ recently ___________ (launch) a new range of lipsticks with the slogan 'we make the feminine life colourful'.

12. Once upon a time there was a man who ___________ (know) nobody better than himself.

13. Jack is such friend of mine who ___________ (make) his mark even in Hollywood.

14. As soon as the thief ___________ (see) the policeman he took to his heels.

15. It is too late now. You ought to ___________ (finish) it before this noon.

16. I ___________ not ___________ (finish), yet.

17. A couple of years ago, he ___________ (be) a poor man who ___________ (have) nothing to offer to others. But now, he ___________ (earn) so much that he can buy the London city if anybody comes to him with such an offer.

18. Many books on that subject ___________ already (appear) in the current year.

19. I ___________ never ___________ (think) of becoming a doctor.

20. During the last year he ___________ (seem) to be gaining ground gradually. But now he ___________ (go) totally out of the arena.

The Past Perfect Tense

The Past Perfect Tense is used:

1 *to express the completion of an action in the past.*

(i) It had stopped snowing.

(ii) Her book had been found.

2 *to express a completed action in past along with a subsequent action.*

(i) She had started her car for office when I crossed the main road.

(ii) The train had steamed off before I reached the station.

(iii) They had left the place before I reached there.
(iv) He told me that his father had flown to Germany.
(v) As soon as she had completed her speech, the people clapped for her.
(vi) When I reached John's house, he had already gone to the playground.

Exercise 4

Fill in the blanks with the Simple Past Tense or The Past Perfect Tense of the verbs given in brackets.

1. As soon as I ___________ (rub) my car clean I ___________ (go) out of the house to have short walk.
2. It ___________ (not make) any sense to run through the muddy streets that time in the evening. So, all the children ___________ (decide) to go back home.
3. When I ___________ (reach) the hall, the party ___________ (be) already over. So, I had to return home without dinner.
4. It was years when we ___________ (see) each other at the Hotel York in New York. Then her austere simplicity ___________ (impress) me awfully.
5. The patient ___________ (die) before the doctor ___________ (reach) the hospital.
6. She ___________ already ___________ (inform) about the death of her grandpa. For that she ___________ (not pay) much attention to what I ___________ (say).
7. By the time we ___________ (get) there, nobody ___________ (come) to attend the meeting.
8. Last week he ___________ (promise) to give me a new pen but later on I ___________ (come) to know that he ___________ already ___________ (make) such promises to many other students in the class.
9. The flight ___________ (take off) before I ___________ (reach) the airport.
10. Last night a thief ___________ (break into) my neighbours' house. When the owner ___________ (wake up), the thief ___________ already ___________ (go) away with the cash.
11. As soon as she ___________ (switch off) the computer, she would play with us.
12. I ___________ already ___________ (take) my dinner when they ___________ (call on) us.
13. The boy ___________ (tell) me that his father was innocent as he ___________ (not commit) any crime.
14. A squirrel ___________ (tunnel) through the hollow trunk of the tree. When the kingfisher ___________ (go) inside the hollow, it ___________ (find) that the squirrel ___________ (be) already there.

The Present Perfect Continuous and The Past Perfect Continuous Tense

A. *If an action has been going on continuously over a period of time and is still going on, the Present Perfect Continuous Tense is used.*

Examples

(i) It has been snowing for two hours.

(ii) She has been living in this house since 1999.

B. *If an action had been going on continuously over a period of time and was still going on at the time of speaking in past, the Past Perfect Continuous Tense is used.*

Examples

(i) He had been working at the airport for twenty years.

(ii) She had been suffering from some intractable disease for ten years when cholera broke out in the city.

(iii) Jack had been watering the plants for three hours when I went to see him.

Exercise 5

Fill in the blanks with Present Perfect Continuous or Past Perfect Continuous Tense.

1. Rose ____________ (operate) the computer since this morning.
2. Tina ____________ (live) in the same house for ten years when she was married to an ambassador.
3. Rita ____________ (draw) pictures since morning with his sketch pen when he returned home.
4. Mrs Maria ____________ (learn) dancing since she was a little girl.

The Simple Future Tense

The Simple Future Tense is used:

1. *to express a future plan.*
   (i) We'll install a new water purifier in our house.
   (ii) They'll get their eye sight checked.
   (iii) I'll meet you tomorrow.
2. *to express an action in future.*
   (i) I'll type a letter this evening.
   (ii) She'll get her bicycle repaired.

3. *In some of the clauses containing if, unless, since, as soon as, until, when, before, after, as long as, in case, while, till, etc. generally Future Tense is not used. In these clauses usually Present Tense is used to give the sense of future.*

(i) Unless you explain to me the whole matter, you won't leave this place.

(ii) If you walk fast, you'll catch the train.

(iii) Don't go until I come back.

(iv) The bride will have got her makeup done before the marriage-party arrives.

(v) He'll be composing a new song when we reach his house.

(vi) The thief will start running as soon as he sees the policeman.

(vii) She will dance after the guests go.

(viii) You must bring an umbrella in case it rains.

(ix) She will not listen to her elders when she is so careless.

(x) Since you do not go for a walk, you will do some exercise at home.

The Future Continuous Tense

The Future Continuous Tense is used *to express an action in progress in future.*

(i) She'll be flying by the British Airlines aeroplane.

(ii) Albert will be counting the gunny bags that he has to send to the Railway Authorities by the end of the month.

(iii) They will be cutting the brown leaves of the plants while we shall be applying the required quantity of manure to the plants in the lawn.

The Future Perfect Tense

The Future Perfect Tense is used *to express the finishing of an action in the future.*

(i) Johnny will have whitewashed the house before being able to arrange a worker.

(ii) The bowing 002 will have taken off when you reach the airport.

(iii) In 2005 he will have been here for fifteen years.

(iv) By this time she will have got her name struck off the roll for being absent continuously for a week.

Future Perfect Continuous Tense

The Future Perfect Continuous Tense is used *to express an activity which will continue over a period of time that will end in future.*

(i) John will have been gathering flowers for two hours to make a garland.

(ii) Lily will have been hacking off the dead shoots and twigs of the plants since morning.

(iii) The children will have been playing for three hours when you reach the playground.

Exercise 6

Fill in the blanks with the correct form of Future and/or Simple Present Tense.

1. He ___________ (sing) a song for five minutes when the guests ___________ (arrive).
2. Alice ___________ (paint) the picture since morning.
3. Daisy___________ (wash) the clothes before you ___________ (reach) her house.
4. John ___________ (tell) a story when you ___________ (reach) there.
5. Mary ___________ (decorate) her room for two hours.
6. ___________ James ___________ (receive) the award for his invention?
7. Lolita ___________ (not go) anywhere until I ___________ (come) back.
8. You ___________ (not leave) these premises as long as I ___________ (be) here.
9. If Maya___________ (prepare) all the accounts of the company by the end of this month we ___________ (submit) the same at once to the authority concerned .
10. You ___________ (be) in the good books of your teacher, if you ___________ (work) hard and ___________ (stand) first in the class.
11. Ruby ___________ (knit) a sweater for her husband for one week when you go to see her next month.
12. Sam___________ (learn) from his uncle the art of making a flower chart on computer since morning.
13. You _______________ (get) a master key of the office in case you ___________ (lose) the original one.
14. You ___________ never ___________ (get) success in your life because you ___________ (be) very lazy.

UNIT 6

TENSES IN CONDITIONAL SENTENCES

I. (i) If it rains, we should not go out of the house.
(ii) If you are coming, I shall wait for you.
(iii) If you have finished your homework, we shall go to visit the Super Market.
(iv) If you have been working for five hours, you shall take some rest.
(v) If you work hard, you will stand first in the class.

II. (i) If you lived near the office, you would never be late.
(ii) If I had time, I should come to see you.
(iii) If you had a screwer, you would be able to fasten and unfasten the bolts.

III. (i) If you had run fast, you would have won the race. (certainty)
(ii) If you had run fast, you could have won the race. (ability)
(iii) If you had run fast, you might have won the race. (possibility)
(iv) If the weather had been fine, they would have come to see us.

IV. (i) If I were you, I would not let him know our secrets.
(ii) If I were the Prime Minister, I would be respected by all.
(iii) If I had been you, I should not have allowed him to talk to me like that.
(iv) What would have happened if the bus had been in collision with the truck?

V. *Miscellaneous structures*

a. If my brother were here **Or** were my brother here
b. If we had not **Or** had we not
c. Should you find the broken eggs

(i) Were my brother here, we would go for a picnic.
(ii) Were your father at home, you would ask him for money to celebrate your birthday.
(iii) Had we set off earlier, we would have reached our destination by now.
(iv) Had we not cut all the trees, we should not have faced such devastating floods.
(v) Should you find the broken eggs in any of the trays being supplied to you, you must contact me at 4050451.

Exercise 1

Fill in the blanks with the correct forms of verbs given in brackets.

1. If I ____________ (be) you, I would not lend him any money.
2. If Selena ____________ (read) the letter properly, she would not have forgotten her aunt's address.
3. If there ____________ (be) no sea storm, no boats would have been wrecked.
4. If you ____________ (have) time, you would go to see the movie.
5. If she ____________ (put on) a spotless dress, she would win the fancy dress competition.
6. ____________ (be) my sister here, we would go to Shimla to spend this summer vacation.
7. ____________ (shall) you get the shirts unironed, you must ask the washerman to iron them.
8. ____________ (have) the troops had a retreat, they would not have been killed.
9. If you had paid close attention to your teachers, you ____________ (get) pass marks.
10. If I ____________ (be) you, I would not have crossed the road so carelessly.
11. What would have happened to the ship if it ____________ (not anchor) at the right time.
12. If she ____________ (brush) her teeth daily, she would have escaped the tooth infection.
13. ____________ I ____________ (place) all my toys in the box, your brother would not have stolen any of them.
14. If he had not crawl out from under the debris, he ____________ (die) of suffocation.
15. If I ____________ (be) you, I would not drive the car at a breakneck speed.
16. ____________ he ____________ (not tasted) coffee, he would not have drunk it.
17. If I ____________ (be) you, I would let the boys make a noise.
18. If the gardener ____________ (have) a trimmer, he would finish trimming earlier.
19. If only we ____________ (have) five minutes late, we would not have caught the flight.
20. If I had not been so busy, I ____________ (attend) the guests properly.

Exercise 2

Rewrite the following conditional sentences according to the pattern given in the first sentence.

1. If he ran fast, he would catch the train.

   If he had run fast he would have caught the train.

2. If I were a doctor, I would not charge any fee from the poor.

   ____

3. If I flew an aeroplane, I would be more alert.

   ____

4. If I had more money, I would buy a big car.

   ____

5. If my brother got an exotic pen, he would write fast and neatly.

   ____

6. If my aunt baked a cake, she would beat the egg and butter properly.

   ____

7. If I were the Prime Minister, I would not allow my neighbours to make nuclear weapons.

   ____

   ____

8. If I were a dress designer, I would stitch only the children's dresses.

   ____

9. If you played the piano, you would enthral the audience.

   ____

10. If you smoked too much, you would fall a victim to some dangerous disease.

    ____

    ____

UNIT 7

MODALS (AUXILIARIES)

Modals are also said to be **Helping Verbs/**

The following are commonly used Modal Auxiliaries :

shall	should	can	could
will	would	may	might
must	must not	used to	ought to
need	need not (needn't)		

Modal Auxiliaries are used in the following ways:

SHALL

1. 'Shall' is used in the first person:

   (a) *to express simple future tense.*

   (i) I shall not bind myself by signing this document.

   (ii) We shall talk about it later on.

   (b) *to express suggestion.*

   (i) Shall I give the car a wash?

   (ii) Shall we start running?

2. 'Shall' is used with the second and third persons:

   (a) *to express a threat.*

   (i) The naughty boys shall be punished.

   (ii) Those who violate the law shall be put behind the bars.

   (b) *to express prohibition.*

   (i) You shall not tell a lie.

   (ii) You shall not drink here.

   (c) *to express legal obligation.*

   (i) You shall pay your income tax before the end of this month.

   (ii) You shall submit your account books in the Sales Tax Office by the due date.

(d) *to express willingness, determination, etc.*
   (i) You shall win the match.
   (ii) He shall not open the box.

SHOULD

'Should' is used:

1. *as past tense of 'shall' in the indirect speech.*
   (i) She told me that I should not walk barefoot.
   (ii) Romy said that they should explore Europe soon.
2. *to express caution, etc.*
   (i) Don't walk on the edge of the canal lest you should fall in it.
   (ii) Don't laugh lest you should be punished.
3. *to express duty, advice, suggestion, etc.*
   (i) You should take an umbrella because there can be rain anytime.
   (ii) You should do your duty honestly.
   (iii) Should I open the window?
   (iv) Should I bring a coffee for you?
4. *to express guess, assumption, etc.*
   (i) It should be 4 pm.
   (ii) This shirt should cost $100.

WILL

'Will' is used:

1. *to express simple future tense with second and third persons.*
   (i) You will break six eggs and then put some sugar in it.
   (ii) He will look into the matter for being a reputed member of the detective agency.
2. *to express general as well as habitual truth.*
   (i) The earth will revolve round the sun.
   (ii) My brother will take a glass of juice in the morning.
3. *to express a request.*
   (i) Will you please lend me your book for a day?
   (ii) Will you guide me to Hotel Park?
4. *to express order.*
   (i) You will do as you are advised.
   (ii) Will you stop laughing?

5. *to express invitation.*
   (i) Will you come to see us tomorrow?
   (ii) Will you join us for the picnic?

6. *to express probability.*
   (i) The weather will break soon.
   (ii) It will rain any time.

Note : Sometimes 'will' is used with first person:

1. *to express determination.*
   (i) I will definitely beat the previous record.
   (ii) I will win the match by hook or by crook.

2. *to express a threat.*
   (i) I will not spare him.
   (ii) I will teach him a lesson.

3. *to express refusal.*
   (i) I won't lend you money any more.
   (ii) I won't allow this dog to enter my house.

WOULD

'Would' is used:

1. *as a past tense of 'will'.*
   (i) He said that he would not run barefoot on the hot sandy beach.
   (ii) She told me that she would not like the idea of sailing on a raft.

2. *to express a wish.*
   (i) Would that I were rich!
   (ii) Would that I were a king!

3. *to make a polite request.*
   (i) Would you please lend me your bicycle for an hour?
   (ii) Would you please help me solve this problem?

4. *to make polite invitation.*
   (i) Would you dine with us tonight?
   (ii) Would you join us in our visit to Shimla?

5. *to express determination.*
   (i) I would get 100 per cent marks.
   (ii) I would give up all my bad habits.

6. *to express an imaginary or unreal condition.*
   - (i) Had you mentioned it before, you would not have been treated so rudely.
   - (ii) If you had worked hard, you would have got pass marks at least.

CAN

'Can' is used:

1. *to express present capability, ability, etc.*
   - (i) He can speak both French and English equally well.
   - (ii) He can drive fast on the Highways.
2. *to make a request.*
   - (i) Can I use your pen?
   - (ii) Can I ask you for help?
3. *to express permission.*
   - (i) You can go now.
   - (ii) You can use my umbrella.

COULD

'Could' is used:

1. *as the past tense of 'can'.*
   - (i) She told me that she could write in German.
   - (ii) He said that he could climb the coconut tree.
2. *to express past capability, ability, etc.*
   - (i) He could give a good fight to his opponent when he was young.
   - (ii) She could sew shirts very well when she was young.
3. *to make a polite request.*
   - (i) Could I use your phone?
   - (ii) Could I read this magazine of yours?

> **Note : 'Could' expresses more politeness than 'Can'.**

MAY

'May' is used:

1. *to express a wish or prayer or curse.*
   - (i) May you get good marks!

(ii) May God help you!

(iii) May you go blind!

2. *to express a strong possibility.*

(i) It may snow today.

(ii) He may be angry with you.

(iii) There may be a snake somewhere around.

3. *to seek permission.*

(i) May I go to toilet, sir?

(ii) May I come in, sir?

4. *to give permission.*

(i) Yes, you may go.

(ii) You may go for lunch.

5. *to express help, service, etc.*

(i) May I help you go across the road?

(ii) May I carry this bag to the room for you?

MIGHT

'Might' is used:

1. *as the past tense of 'may':*

(i) She told me that her brother might come home that day.

(ii) The boy asked me if he might use my pen.

2. *to express remote possibility.*

(i) There are small patches of clouds sailing in the sky. It might rain in the evening.

(ii) He might contact you at 10 pm.

Note : 'Might' expresses less possibility than 'may'.

3. *to seek permission or to give permission.*

(i) Might I go out for tea?

(ii) You might go.

Note : 'Might' is more polite than 'may' but 'may' is more frequently used.

MUST

'Must' is used:

1. *to express strong possibility.*
   (i) He must deliver his maiden speech today.
   (ii) It must rain tonight.
2. *to express compulsion.*
   (i) You must go to Canada to see your uncle.
   (ii) You must finish your homework by the evening.
3. *to express obligation, duty, etc.*
   (i) We must love our countrymen.
   (ii) You must obey your parents.

> **Note : 'Ought to' is the most suitable modal to express moral obligation.**

4. *to give advice.*
   (i) You must brush your hair before leaving the house.
   (ii) You must polish your shoes daily.
5. *to express determination.*
   (i) I must cross the English Channel today.
   (ii) I must earn a lot of money in a few years.

MUSTN'T (MUST NOT)

'Mustn't is used *to express obligation, compulsion, etc.*

(i) You mustn't touch my toys.
(ii) You mustn't sing here otherwise the baby may break from the sleep.
(iii) You mustn't stand here at night.
(iv) You mustn't come home late.

OUGHT TO

'Ought to' is used:

1. *to express moral duty.*
   (i) You ought to help the needy.
   (ii) You ought to do something good to mankind.

2. *to express obligation.*
   - (i) You ought to respect your elders.
   - (ii) You ought to obey your teachers.

3. *to express advice or suggestion.*
   - (i) If you don't like this drink, you ought to ask for something else.
   - (ii) You ought to see a doctor at once.

NEED

'Need' is used *to express obligation, necessity, etc. It is used in Interrogative sentences.*

- (i) Need I request you again?
- (ii) Need I remind you about it once again?

NEEDN'T (NEED NOT)

'Needn't' is used *to express obligation, necessity.*

- (i) You needn't poke your nose in our affairs.
- (ii) You needn't bring your bags tomorrow.

USED TO

'Used to' is used:

1. *to express some habit in the past.*
   - (i) He used to smoke when his parents were out.
   - (ii) She used to talk to herself when she grew old.
2. *to express present habit.*
   - (i) I am not used to talking about others' shortcomings.
   - (ii) He is not used to getting up early in the morning.
3. *to show the existence of something in the past.*
   - (i) There used to be an oak tree in the garden.
   - (ii) There used to be a three star hotel in the city.

HAVE TO

'Have to' is used *to express compulsion, obligation, etc.*

- (i) You have to work hard.
- (ii) You have to run fast otherwise you won't reach the station on time.
- (iii) You have to go to the post office right now.

HAD TO

'Had to' is the past tense of 'have to' and is used *to express obligation, compulsion, necessity, etc.*

(i) She had to leave her job for the sake of her dignity.

(ii) He had to accept the charges against him.

(iii) They had to leave their country for a respectable job.

DARE

'Dare' is used *to express courageousness. It is used in interrogative sentences.*

(i) How dare you talk to me like this?

(ii) How dare you search my pockets?

DAREN'T (DARE NOT)

'Daren't' is used *to express lack of courageousness.*

(i) He daren't ask me anything about it.

(ii) He daren't shoot me a look at all.

(iii) He daren't have a duel with me.

Exercise 1

Fill in the blanks with suitable auxiliaries.

1. ____________ you speak German? No, I ____________ . But I ____________ speak English well.
2. You ____________ go now and please send the next candidate in.
3. Her brother ____________ smoke heavily. But he has stopped smoking now.
4. You ____________ arrange these flowers in the vase because I ____________ do this job in a better manner than you.
5. He was beaten black and blue by me but he ____________ not complain against me to the teacher.
6. This old man ____________ lift this stone but he ____________ lift a stone even heavier than this one when he was young.
7. You ____________ beat this egg and butter right now because your papa wants something to eat at the earliest.
8. You ____________ touch my books otherwise they ____________ get spoiled.

9. ____________ you like to join us to Switzerland this summer vacation?

10. ____________ that I were a billionaire!

11. If you don't like these dishes you ____________ to ask for something else.

12. The sky is overcast with clouds and it ____________ rain anytime.

13. Jack has torn my book. I ____________ spare him.

14. I ____________ check your bag before you leave these premises.

15. ____________ God bless you!

16. I ____________ stand by you through thick and thin.

17. This road ____________ remain closed to traffic for two days.

18. ____________ I use you pen? Yes, you ____________ .

19. There ____________ to be a squarish garden on the corner of the street but now you ____________ find a hotel there.

20. I ____________ solve this sum in no time but your brother ____________ because he is weak in mathematics. Oh, I see. Then he ____________ pay much more attention to this subject because it is one such subject in which you ____________ score full marks.

21. You ____________ give any advice because you don't have any acquaintance with this sort of jobs.

22. She ____________ to leave her house because her parents hated her and her brothers' behaviour with her wasn't charitable either.

23. ____________ I open the window?

24. ____________ you please dine with us tonight?

25. ____________ I dance with you?

Exercise 2

Tick the correct alternative in each of the following sentences.

1. You needn't / mustn't wait for us for long.
2. Should / will I switch on the Air Conditioner?
3. Should / would you please help me?

4. May / could you succeed in life!
5. Should / could I use your motorbike for a while?
6. She kept abusing him but he dared not / needed not answer her back.
7. May / could I go for lunch now? Yes, you may / should.
8. You ought to / will serve your countrymen.
9. She used to / dared go to bed early in the evening.
10. You will / shall pay your debt by the end of this month.
11. He has to / had to work day and night to earn his livelihood but he could never be a rich man through his life.
12. You should not / shall not run along the fence or you will be punished.
13. You must / need stop talking or I shall / will give you a sound beating.
14. My uncle can / could read both English and German very well. He can / could read French too when he was young.
15. Could / would that I were a rich man!

UNIT 8

CONCORD

The finite verb must agree with the subject.

Examples

(i) Dolly and Julie **are** friends. (two persons)
(ii) Her round and chubby face **makes** her look like a doll.

A. Verb with 'or', 'Neither ----- nor' or 'Either ----- or'

With these conjunctions, the verb should be applied according to the last subject in the sentence.

Examples

(i) Neither fruits nor vegetables **grow** on this land.
(ii) Neither Jack nor his parents **have** been granted permission to leave London.
(iii) Neither boys nor the girl **was** asked to join the marriage party.

(i) Either Lucy or her brothers **have** been assigned this job.
(ii) Either the monkeys or the elephant **has** powers to ask the rabbits such a question.
(iii) Either Tony or Martin **was** found in a state of unconsciousness.

(i) Alex or his friends **have** been appointed members of the committee.
(ii) The boys or the gatekeeper **has** to keep watch around the school's premises.
(iii) Diana or Jane **is** going to attend the crucial meeting at Zambia on 25th of this month.

Exercise 1

Correct the following sentences. If the sentence is already correct, put the tick (✓) mark against it.

1. Neither war nor calmness have given relief to his jumpy nerves.

____

2. Either Lily or Mona has to join the troupe to sing the song in chorus.

____

3. Colin or his friends is going to visit the dog shop.

____

4. Jack or his mother are being approached by the company for finance.

____

5. Neither David nor his relatives was present at the ball.

____

6. Either her friends or Nadia are being called to start the election campaign.

____

7. Neither Peter nor his brother take interest in games.

____

8. Rosy or Nina are to be selected for dance competition.

____

9. Either aunt Mary or Nina have baked this delicious cake.

____

10. Tanks or Jumbo Jet are being sent to the border.

____

B. Some expressions and some nouns (determiner + noun) always take singular verb.

Examples

(i) Measles **has** almost been eradicated from the world.

(ii) Tennis **is** very much popular in western countries.

(iii) Slow and steady **wins** the race.

(iv) Rice and curry **is** my favourite dish.

(v) The latest news **is** that India has become the supreme power in Information Technology.

(vi) The poetry of Keats **is** immortal.

(vii) The scenery of Kashmir **is** unforgettable.

(viii) Each boy **was** sent a message to his parents.

(ix) Every girl **needs** to learn creative arts.

C. Some nouns always take a plural verb.

Examples

(i) Cattle **were** lashed mercilessly.

(ii) These scissors **are** blunt.

(iii) These baggy pants **need** one more course of washing.

(iv) Nancy talks as if she **were** a queen.

D. A collective noun takes a singular verb when it acts as a whole, but it takes a plural verb when two individuals of which it is composed are considered separately.

Examples

(i) The jury **was** unanimous on its decision.

(ii) The jury **have** given their separate opinions in the matter.

E. If the two nouns refer to the same person, the verb should be singular but when they refer to different persons the verb should be plural.

Examples

(i) The black and the brown buffaloes **were** sent to the shed. (two buffaloes)

(ii) The black and white cat **was** caught by the hunter. (one cat)

Exercise 2

Correct the following sentences. If the sentence is already correct put the tick mark (✓) against it.

1. Brick and stone are used to build houses.

____

2. Where are your spectacles?

____

3. The committee was divided on the decision of arrangement of funds.

____

4. The black and the white birds flies high in the sky.

____

5. The fat hen and the thin dog has already lost the race.

____

6. The forceps in the hand of this scientist have been imported from Germany.

____

7. Mumps causes a severe pain on the body parts close to ears.

____

8. The furniture are made up of wood and metal.

____

9. He walks as if he is a king.

____

10. Lily talks as though she is a queen.

____

F. Some expressions take verb according to the first subject.

Examples

(i) Maya along with her parents **was** ready to join the trek to the south.

(ii) Herry as well as his relatives **has** flown to South Africa to see a match between India and the host team.

(iii) Lucy accompanied by her sister feels happy and **is** ready to join the horse riding expedition through the dense forest.

(iv) The boys along with their father **are** trying to invent a new machine, which will enhance the production of copper wires about five folds at less cost.

(v) The cubs accompanied by the lioness **are** going to trap some animal to feast on it.

(vi) The girl as well as her brother **has** climbed the tree to pluck some fresh guavas.

Exercise 3

Correct the following sentences. If the sentence is already correct, put a tick mark (✓).

1. Tina along with her sisters were cordially invited on the auspicious occasion of the marriage of Mrs Mary's daughter.

____

____

2. The children as well as their father have gone to Paris to see the beauty of the Eiffel Tower.

____

____

3. The boys as well as their uncle has been asked to assist the police in their investigation of the case.

____

____

4. The carpenter along with other apprentices have completed the wooden work in time.

____

____

5. The child accompanied by his mother is dancing on the floor on the occasion of the birthday of his sister.

____

____

6. The chickens as well as their mother has been put to feeding grains.

____

____

UNIT 9

CONJUNCTIONS

Conjunctions are used to join two or more sentences, words or phrases.

Examples

(a) Monte could not do much progress in his studies.

(b) Monte did not get much time to read his books.

(a+b) Monte could not do much progress in his studies **because** he did not get much time to read his books.

There are the following kinds of conjunctions:

1. Coordinating Conjunctions
2. Correlative Conjunctions
3. Subordinating Conjunctions
4. Compound Conjunctions

1. **Coordinating Conjunctions** are used to join the sentences or clauses of equal rank.

and	but	neither... nor	either... or
yet	or	not only... but also	

Examples

i. Martin **and** Tony are brothers.
ii. The path was full of rounds and bends **yet** we managed to reach your house.
iii. Work hard **or** you won't get good marks.
iv. He is disabled **but** kind.

2. **Correlative Conjunctions** are used in pairs.

not only... but also	either... or	neither... nor
although... yet	whether...or	

Examples

i. **Neither** Peter **nor** his friends have turned up for the match.
ii. **Either** buy this tea set **or** leave the shop.
iii. **Not only** does she speak English, **but also** she speaks German equally well.

3. **Subordinating Conjunctions** join together a dependent clause and a main clause.

when	since	as	before
after	until	unless	if that
so that	provided that	because	till

The subordinating conjunctions can be classified as under:

A **Subordinating Conjunctions of Time**: until, till, when/while, before, as, since, after

(i) You will not touch anything in the room **until / till** you are allowed to do so.
(ii) Juliet will be back **before** the day breaks.
(iii) The guests arrived **after** we had finished dinner.
(iv) She has been living in this house **since** she was five years old.
(v) Somebody cried **when / while** I was drawing a picture.

B **Subordinating Conjunctions of Place**: where, wherever

(i) Please go **where** you can find good opportunities for progress.
(ii) I shall find you out **wherever** you may go.

C **Subordinating Conjunctions of Purpose**: lest, that, so that

(i) Walk slowly **lest** you should fall.
(ii) We eat **that** we may live.
(iii) My father works day and night **so that** he may earn a handsome amount.

D **Subordinating Conjunctions of Cause / Reason**: as, since, because

(i) She is weeping bitterly **as** she has lost her purse.
(ii) **Since** he had been bitten by a dog he did not come to attend the meeting.
(iii) Jack was admitted to a local hospital **because** he had his leg broken.

E **Subordinating Conjunctions of Condition**: unless, provided that, if

(i) You won't be allowed to board the train **unless** you show me the ticket.
(ii) **If** you pull the rope with more force it'll snap.
(iii) I'll lend you the book **provided that** you return it to me by the end of this month.

F **Subordinating Conjunctions of Result:** so, that

(i) He set off on the journey before the daybreak, **so** he reached Hong Kong before 9 am.
(ii) He was so busy **that** he could not attend to me.

G **Subordinating Conjunctions of Comparison / Concession**

Comparison ⟶ than, as
Concession ⟶ Although, though

(i) She is fatter **than** you (are).
(ii) He is as weak **as** you are.

(iii) I love him **though** he hates me.
(iv) I don't like meat **although** it is good for health.

4. **Compound Conjunctions** are the phrases, which are used to join together two or more clauses.

as if...	in order to	as soon as	as well as	even if

Examples

(i) He takes **as if** he were the king.
(ii) **As soon as** the child saw the clown he cried loudly.
(iii) **In order to** reach at the Airport on time, Mr John started walking fast.

Exercise 1

Join the following sentences using Coordinating Conjunctions.

1. (a) Rosy is going to America tonight.
   (b) Dolly is going to America tonight.

   ____

2. (a) Danny will not be sanctioned leave for a week.
   (b) Henry will not be sanctioned leave for a week.

   ____

   ____

3. (a) Clip the hedges of my lawn.
   (b) Leave the place.

   ____

4. (a) The newspaper was full of glaring errors.
   (b) David understood it all.

   ____

5. (a) Put manure to the plants soon.
   (d) The plants may wither.

   ____

6. (a) Our landlord is rich.
   (b) Our landlord is unkind.

   ____

7. (a) John knows dancing well.
   (b) John knows singing well.

____

8. (a) It was an old ramshackle.
   (b) I managed to drive it to the garage.

____

9. (a) My watch is out of order.
   (b) The watch of my sister is working properly.

____

____

10. (a) The clouds of smoke were emerging from the chimney.
    (b) They were slowly engulfing the entire atmosphere over the area.

____

____

Exercise 2

Fill in the blanks with a suitable Conjunction.

1. ____________ you had listened to your father, you would have succeeded in life. (unless, until, if)
2. ____________ the child saw the snake, he raised an alarm. (as long as, as soon as)
3. ____________ winter begins migratory birds will fly away to warmer countries. (when, that, because).
4. Look sharp ____________ you should miss the flight. (in case, lest, so)
5. ____________ you put on those black baggy trousers and a white silk shirt, you will look like a dandy. (until, unless, if).
6. You must dial us ____________ you lose your ATM card. (in case, that, as).
7. ____________ you are not going to attend the meeting, you must give a helping hand to your wife. (as soon as, as long as, since).
8. I'll start arranging furniture in the hall ____________ the guests arrive. (provided that, before).
9. A mail train was derailed ____________ it collided with a stationary goods train. (after, unless, until)

10. She gave us elaborate description of the place __________ she was asked about it. (when, that, so that)

11. You won't go anywhere __________ I come back. (provided that, until)

12. She tried her best to go deep into the matter, __________ she could not find out any good reason for her father's short temper. (in case, but, although)

13. You can't get into shape __________ you start taking light exercise every morning. (provided that, in case, unless)

14. I'll lend you my umbrella __________ you return it to me by the evening. (provided that, unless, until)

Exercise 3

Join each of the pairs of the following sentences to form one sentence.

1. (a) The arrow pierced his heart.
   (b) He was sitting in his chair. (while)

   ____

   ____

2. (a) Hands off this yummy cake.
   (b) You'll be scolded by Mary. (or)

   ____

   ____

3. (a) The cobbler demanded a box of dubbin.
   (b) He wanted to soften leather. (since)

   ____

   ____

4. (a) The sun rises.
   (b) Its alpenglow spreads over the distant mountains. (and)

   ____

   ____

5. (a) She could not set aside any money for future.
   (b) She was extravagant. (because)

   ____

   ____

6. (a) He was asked to choose from a great many old articles.
   (b) He took a highly burnished steel cap which belonged to her grandpapa, Colonel Wood. (when)

____

____

7. (a) You won't indulge in gossip.
   (b) You have to finish your homework before sunset. (because)

____

____

8. (a) Her knowledge put the adroit workforce of the company to shame.
   (b) She was immediately offered a high post in the company. (so)

____

____

9. (a) He realized that he was lacking in the necessary academic qualities to be taken as a university scholar.
   (b) He started taking interest in film industry. (as)

____

____

10. (a) She can't go abroad.
    (b) She has to get her visa from the MEA. (until)

____

____

11. (a) The roads of Singapore were cleared of all traffic.
    (b) The caravans of Ambassadors from almost all corners of the world were about to pass. (as)

____

____

UNIT 10

PREPOSITIONS

Read the following sentences.

(i) The Prime Minister arrived **at** International Airport this morning.
(ii) Jane was extremely poor **at** studies.

A Preposition joins the noun with the rest of the sentence.

There are following kinds of Prepositions:

1. Prepositions of Place
2. Prepositions of Time
3. Prepositions of Method, Instrumentality
4. Prepositions of Cause, Reason, Purpose
5. Prepositions of Manner
6. Prepositions of Rate, Measurement and Quantity
7. Prepositions of Contrast, Concession
8. Prepositions of Possession

1. Prepositions of Place

in	on	at	in front of
behind	across	over	along
through	above	below	under
beside			

Examples

(i) Her house is **on** the corner of the street.
(ii) We had lunch **at** hotel Plaza.
(iii) The train arrived **at** platform number 9.
(iv) I saw him standing **at** the local bus stop just before the hospital.
(v) My brother lives **in** California but my sister lives **at** Yosemite, a small village.
(vi) My uncle works **in** a toy shop. (the kind of place)
(vii) My aunt works **at** J.K decorators. (the name of an organization)
(viii) I read this news **in** the newspaper **in** the taxi **on** my way home.
(ix) She put the papers **in** her bag and shut its mouth.
(x) There was a lamp post **in front of** the house.
(xi) My friend lives **across / over** the highway.

(xii) We walked a long way **along** the fence.
(xiii) She went **across** the floor. (a flat surface)
(xiv) She brought her hand **over** her eyes. (covering and touching the eyes)
(xv) She brought her hand **above** her head. (not touching the head)
(xvi) He elbowed his way **through** the crush.
(xvii) He was standing **below** the level of the table **on** the platform.
(xviii) She hid her paper **under** the bedsheet.
(xix) She sat **beside** her granny.

Exercise 1

Fill in the blanks with Prepositions of Place.

1. My friend's father works ____________ M/s L.G. Electronics.
2. My cousin works ____________ a bank ____________ America.
3. There was a name-plate ____________ the door of the house bearing the name of the owner.
4. He brought his hand ____________ his brow in disappointment.
5. There was a big house ____________ the corner of the street. Inside the house, there was a spacious well-decorated room ____________ one corner and inside the room there was a round table ____________ which a bunch of keys was lying.
6. He met me ____________ the bus stop. He was wearing a pair of faded jeans, a silk shirt and a pair of shiny shoes. In such an outfit, he looked quite attractive.
7. She got ____________ the car and drove off.
8. ____________ the house there was an old oak tree in which numerous birds had built their nests.
9. His mother advised him not to keep anything back from her but he did not obey her and started keeping his comics ____________ the pillow ____________ his bed.
10. She sat ____________ the chair ____________ her bed and kept singing songs till she got asleep.
11. An ashy gigantic figure moved ____________ the floor in a flash.
12. The horse broke loose and began to run ____________ the fence.
13. The squirrel tunnelled ____________ the hollow trunk of the tree.
14. He brought his hand ____________ his head and waved at his friend who was about to get ____________ the bus.
15. She put the books ____________ the bag, and shut it.

2. Prepositions of Time

at	in	on	until/till
throughout	by	from	during
for	before	after	over

Examples

(i) It was a dark night. All was serene around but **at** 12o'clock a tinkle in the adjacent room woke me up.
(ii) He worked in this office **from** 1980 to 2000.
(iii) Lily was born **at** 5 pm **on** Monday **in** the month of January **in** 1999.
(iv) My uncle will return to India **by** the end of this year.
(v) **During** his journey, he read three books.
(vi) **In** summer, **during** the post-morning hours, the sun beats down brightly.
(vii) I'll wait for you **until** the evening.
(viii) He remained a recluse **throughout** his life.
(ix) Please wait **for** a moment.
(x) We reached Dubai **before** day-break.
(xi) They left that place **after** Christmas.
(xii) The patient has been recovering **over** the past few hours.

Exercise 2

Fill in the blanks with Prepositions of Time.

1. __________ the day time it rained heavily.
2. She had to work hard __________ her life.
3. John remained a leading biologist __________ 1990 to 2010.
4. I would manage to reach my uncle's __________ 9o'clock.
5. We stopped at the bus stop __________ a few minutes.
6. My sister was born __________ 10 pm __________ Sunday __________ November __________ 1987.
7. He had enjoyed himself __________ his life but a few days __________ dying he felt ashamed of his misdeeds.
8. The Superfast Express arrived at the station __________ time.
9. I'm sure he will definitely tell us the secret but we have to wait __________ noon.
10. __________ the end of this month, he will have earned about one million dollars.
11. __________ Christmas nobody saw him anywhere.

12. The weather has been recovering __________ the past few days.

13. He worked as the Chief Engineer __________ 2008 to 2012.

14. The flight took off __________ time and the aeroplane reached London __________ 8 o'clock.

15. I'll be back __________ sun-set.

3. Prepositions of Method or Instrumentality

Examples

(i) Robert cut the cake **with** a knife.

(ii) The company sends its important documents **by** registered post.

4. Prepositions expressing Cause, reason, purpose

Examples

(i) His aunt died **of** heart attack.

(ii) The old man died **of** pneumonia.

(iii) His mother died **from** overwork.

(iv) The girl saw the lion and began to tremble **with** fear.

(v) Nelson Mandela struggled **for** freedom of South Africa.

(vi) Smoking is injurious **to** health.

5. Prepositions expressing Possession.

Examples

(i) This book belongs **to** Henry.

(ii) The boy **with** black curly hair is my friend.

Exercise 3

Fill in the blanks with the Prepositions expressing instruments, possession, cause, reason or purpose.

1. Robert is a man __________ word.
2. The man __________ black hair is John's uncle.
3. The girl __________ curly hair is suffering __________ pneumonia.
4. The children __________ school uniform draw sketches __________ amusement.
5. The woman __________ blue eyes is struggling __________ livelihood.

6. I heard this news through one __________ my relatives.
7. The woodcutter cut down the tree __________ an axe __________ a jigsaw edge.
8. The child __________ short hair lost his bag __________ negligence.
9. The envelope __________ its corners coloured __________ blue was sent to Mr David __________ registered post.
10. The snake charmer aroused the snake __________ beating out a sweet tune.
11. The kettle __________ a long handle is boiling on the stove.
12. The house __________ Mr Paul is luxurious though it lies along the hillside.
13. This pen belongs __________ Adam and he daily writes a letter __________ it.
14. Cholera is spread __________ germs, which are found in contaminated food and liquids.
15. Many truck loads of apples were sent to Bombay __________ trains.

6. Prepositions of Manner, Contrast, Concession, Degree, Rate, Measure, Quantity etc.

(i) Cloth is sold **by** the metre. (manner)
(ii) The boy jumped into the river **with** great courage. (manner)
(iii) **In spite** of his best efforts, he could not pass the examination. (contrast)
(iv) This city is situated about 5000 metres **above** the sea level. (quantity)

Exercise 4

Fill in the blanks with Prepositions expressing Manner, Contrast, Concession, Degree, Quantity, Rate, etc.

1. He is nothing __________ a fool of the first water.
2. My uncle has a collection __________ 5000 stamps.
3. __________ of his being honest he could not prove his innocence.
4. Oil is sold __________ the litre.
5. Johnny killed the snake __________ a rod __________ great courage.
6. The train was running __________ the speed of 175 km/hr.
7. The fox jumped again and again __________ in vain.
8. England lost the final match __________ two wickets.

9. Give me five dozens __________ bananas and pack them in a basket.

10. She tried hard to elevate herself to a level __________ the common society.

11. Tina picked the hamper and walked out of the house to buy mangoes, which are sold __________ the kilo. She also wanted to buy some snacks, which are sold __________ packets.

12. The thieves were beaten badly __________ rods by the villagers and later on two of them died __________ over-bleeding in the hospital.

13. __________ her running so fast she could not catch the bus which was being driven __________ the speed of 100 km/hr.

14. His aunt wrote __________ 40 books on cookery.

15. The old man was dying __________ inches.

Exercise 5

Tick the correct Preposition.

1. My house is situated __________ the corner of the street.
   a) in　　b) on　　c) at

2. There is a small but beautiful lawn __________ the corner of my house.
   a) in　　b) on　　c) at

3. I got up __________ 6 o'clock and saw the rosy light of the sun spreading over the distant hills.
   a) at　　b) on　　c) with

4. The chef cut the meat into slices __________ a sharp knife.
   a) on　　b) with　　c) from

5. I visited the zoo three times __________ 1989-2004.
   a) on　　b) since　　c) between

6. Milk is sold __________ the litre.
   a) by　　b) with　　c) for

7. This organization consists __________ five hundred members.
   a) of　　b) with　　c) on

8. Alex ran fast __________ the road as he wanted to catch the bus.
   a) upon　　b) across　　c) with

9. Dolly ran __________ the bus and she caught it in the end.
   a) after　　b) over　　c) from

10. There is a big tree __________ my house, in which the birds sit and chirp all the day.
a) after b) on c) in front of

11. My uncle lives __________ Switzerland which is known for its scenic beauty and chocolates.
a) at b) on c) in

12. I met him __________ the hotel Ritz where he had come to receive his friend.
a) at b) on c) upon

13. Peter never wants to be civilized because the modern society is based __________ money and it is something Peter hates the most.
a) on b) at c) with

14. She sat __________ her mother in a chair.
a) besides b) beside c) across

15. We sailed a boat __________ the river in the moonlight.
a) on b) above c) through

16. My uncle started dividing the sweets __________ the children but he realized his folly when after sometime the room went crowded with brats.
a) among b) between c) by

17. I will return home __________ four days.
a) within b) after c) on

18. Sophia was born __________ a royal family, still she did not boast of her wealth.
a) with b) of c) from

19. One night I saw a strange bird flying __________ my house beating its wings very slowly.
a) over b) upon c) on

20. There is an electric break-down and the authorities say that __________ 11 o'clock they would be able to supply it again.
a) for b) by c) in

21. Jack is senior __________ me in age.
a) than b) from c) to

22. We searched his room __________ the secret documents but found nothing incriminating.
a) on b) for c) with

23. The five troops walked forward and broke open the door __________ courage.
a) for b) with c) in

24. She took hold of the bowl __________ tongs.
a) with b) on c) to

25. His uncle died __________ typhoid for having not been treated in time.
a) of b) from c) on

26. The London Express arrived at the station __________ time.
a) upon b) after c) on

27. My friend's father works __________ Ms S Brown and Co.
a) at b) on c) in

28. __________ the bank of the canal there was an old oak tree.
a) in b) on c) with

29. Robert was born __________ the month of March.
a) in b) on c) over

30. Drinking is injurious __________ health.
a) to b) in c) upon

Some phrases take a particular Preposition to convey a particular sense.

agree with a person
agree to someone's proposal
apply to someone
apply for a post
blind in/of one eye
blind to someone's misdeeds
apologize to someone
apologize for misconduct
deal in sugar, etc.
deal with a person, customers, etc.
in a polite, harsh manner, etc.
complain against somebody
complain to someone
angry at somebody's bad behaviour, etc.
angry with somebody
accuse of theft, etc.
charge with murder, etc.
differ from (appearance)
differ with someone in opinion
brood over
take off shoes, etc.
put on shoes etc.
take after (resemble)
alert to some problem, etc.
blame for

allocate/allot to someone
alternate with
alternative to
adapt to circumstances, etc.
adapt from a novel, etc.
adept at a skill
admit to reality
admit for delay, etc.
adjourn to a hotel, etc.
adjourn to a next date, etc.
adjust for
adjust to
affiliate to/with
afraid of dogs, etc.
aim at
arrange with
arrange in rows, etc.
arrange for
ascend to a level
ashamed of
assault (N) on
associated with
attach to
attack (N) on
attend to
bite into

bless with
beat at
beat on/against
blow on
boast of
bore into
born of
bring about
brood over
fall through
bump into/against
burst with
burst into/out
confident of
deaf of
famous with
famous for
fond of
good at
poor at
weak in
greedy for
faithful to
loyal to
deficient in
open to
shocked at
short of
sorry for
supply to
talk to
wait on
treat with
throw at
search for
submit to
save from
lead to
laugh at
knock at/on
prefer to
protect from
quarrel with
deprive of
abstain from

bite at
sure of
suspicious of
true to
acquit of
appeal to
arrive at
avail (oneself) of
beg for mercy, etc.
beg of
beware of
congratulate on
cure of
die of a disease, etc
die from overwork
dream of
explain to
fall upon
fight for
inquire into
invite to
keep from
laugh at
lack in
look at
object to
protect from
rely on
remind of
rule over
prevent from
protect against
ward off
desirous of
deficient in
devoid of
wonder/marvel at
be surprised at
attend to
pay attention to
absent from
relieve of
dispense with
open to (conviction)
vexed at

refrain from
worthy of
sure of
suspicious of
honest in
fit for
eligible for
familiar to
familiar with
free from
anxious about
averse to
proud/vain of
heed to

instrumental in
insist on
persist in
amazed at
subscribe/ascribe to
contribute to
confident of
assure of
allude to
afflicted with
sympathize with
break in
break out
break into

Exercise 6

Fill in the blanks with suitable Prepositions.

1. A thief broke __________ the house of Mr Brown last night.
2. Being a rich man, Mr Johnson boasts __________ his wealth.
3. Beware __________ these ferocious wild beasts.
4. My uncle deals __________ sugar and he is famous __________ the local public __________ his excellent behaviour and moreover, he deals very politely __________ his customers.
5. I lodged a complaint __________ the postman __________ the postmaster.
6. Everybody congratulated Miss Maria __________ her grand success in the examinations.
7. He abstained __________ smoking.
8. The judge acquitted him __________ all criminal charges.
9. I agree __________ your proposal.
10. She agrees __________ you.
11. She was vexed __________ her failure.
12. He is worthy __________ respect and esteem.
13. Tom was suspicious __________ his brother's dealings.
14. Thomas apologised __________ me __________ his misconduct.

15. They charged the stranger __________ theft.

16. John was true __________ his friends and had established his loyalty.

17. James is weak __________ mathematics but he is good __________ English.

18. She brooded __________ past sorrowful events.

19. Amy was sure __________ her success.

20. He is proud __________ his strength.

21. I prefer coffee __________ tea.

22. My brother has applied __________ the post __________ an officer __________ the chairman __________ the company.

23. Charles Dickens is famous __________ his novels.

24. Gomes is obedient __________ his elders whereas his brother does not heed __________ their advice.

25. Jane is slow __________ speaking whereas his brother Martin, is slow __________ hearing.

26. Max is fond __________ reading novels but his brother takes a keen interest __________ sports.

27. Honey is respectful __________ his parents and he also has a great regard __________ his teachers.

28. Tony belongs __________ a good family and his friend, Jacky also was born __________ a noble family.

29. Ruby was angry __________ you but her sister really thought __________ you as a noble boy.

30. Harry too was angry __________ your downright, rude behaviour.

31. The hotel I lived in for a night was infested __________ rats.

32. At the dead of the night somebody knocked __________ the door.

33. They prevented me __________ going to Singapore.

34. This road leads __________ London.

35. He supplied strategic information __________ the neighbouring country secretly.

36. Jim smiled __________ his follies.

37. We searched the house __________ the lost keys of my chest but in vain.

38. The boy threw a stone _________ the dog, which hit it _________ the head.

39. The passengers were waiting _________ the train anxiously, which was _________ the schedule.

40. The clerk submitted all his documents _________ the officer.

41. Trust _________ God and do the right.

42. She was amazed _________ his candidness and sense of self-respect.

43. Mr Ford is the foremost candidate of this organization; so you should rely _________ him.

44. This place reminds me _________ my own city.

45. You should not laugh _________ others _________ their being inferior _________ you in knowledge.

46. A broad smile played _________ his lips.

47. She is looking _________ her parents with great care and love.

48. I warned him _________ the danger ahead but he did not lend his ears _________ me.

49. All of us rejoice _________ his success.

50. Our company has contributed $ 10000/- _________ the Flood Relief Fund.

51. We should not talk _________ a stranger.

52. This chemical will definitely mix _________ water.

53. Her bag differs _________ mine _________ many ways.

54. Anu took _________ her hair band and put _________ a new one brought by her aunt.

55. The hunter aimed the gun _________ the dove.

56. Victor was ashamed _________ his misconduct and finding it difficult _________ face his father, he left the home.

57. We adjourned _________ a hotel _________ dinner.

58. My school is affiliated _________ the ICSE.

59. His father died _________ cancer whereas the death of his brother was brought _________ by overwork. Earlier, his uncle too had died _________ overwork.

60. You had better wrestle _________ your studies than just whiling _________ your time.

61. _________ the very beginning this piece of land was allocated/ allotted _________ the refugees.

62. Don't talk _________ such a foolish boy.

63. She was confident _________ her success.

64. He was shocked _________ the choice of his wife for such tawdry jewellery.

65. She prohibited her husband _________ drinking and brought home _________ him the harmful effects of it.

66. The brief-case was bursting _________ dirty clothes.

67. He warded _________ his rival's blow deftly.

68. Take this pill, it will soon cure you _________ the disease.

69. Lolita wrote a letter _________ her aunt whom she had never seen.

70. The patient was admitted _________ the hospital.

71. The child bit _________ the cake.

72. This film is adapted _________ a novel.

73. He beat _________ the flames of fire.

74. He blew _________ the hot tea to get it cool fast.

75. He is poor _________ some of the subjects.

76. The dog is greedy _________ meat.

77. She was lacking _________ common sense.

78. In no way am I going to explain it _________ you.

79. These black trousers do not appeal _________ me.

80. The old man heaved himself out of bed and as he moved a short length, he bumped _________ a table.

UNIT 11

ACTIVE AND PASSIVE VOICE

Read the following sentences.

The old man made a lurch at the rope (Active Voice)
A lurch at the rope was made by the old man. (Passive Voice)

A. Passive Voice of Assertive Sentences (Tense-wise)

(i) ***Present Indefinite***

1. Robin examines the slide under the microscope. (Active)
   The slide is examined by Robin under the microscope. (Passive)
2. We propel the boat using paddles. (Active)
   The boat is propelled by us using paddles. Passive)
3. Jimmy does not request anybody for help. (Active)
   Anybody is not requested for help by Jimmy.
   Or, Nobody is requested by Jimmy for help. (Passive)
4. Rocky and his friends do not show much interest in foreign goods. (Active)
   Much interest in foreign goods is not shown by Rocky and his friends. (Passive)

(ii) ***Present Continuous***

1. Mr Harris is operating an old machine. (Active)
   An old machine is being operated by Mr Harris. (Passive)
2. Mrs Clara and her husband are arranging a party on the eve of their twenty-fifth marriage anniversary. (Active)
   A party is being arranged by Mrs Clara and her husband on the eve of their twenty-fifth marriage anniversary. (Passive)
3. Miss Sophia is not cutting the cake into properly squarish slices. (Active)
   The cake is not being cut into properly squarish slices by Miss Sophia. (Passive)
4. Peter and his brothers are not taking the correct weight of the junk articles. (Active)
   The correct weight of the junk articles is not being taken by Peter and his brothers. (Passive)

(iii) ***Present Perfect***

1. Lily has brought her company on a firm footing in just three years. (Active)
   Her company has been brought on a firm footing in just three years by Lily. (Passive)
2. Zenith and her mother have dropped the idea of going abroad. (Active)
   The idea of going abroad has been dropped by Zenith and her mother. (Passive)
3. She hasn't completed her thesis yet. (Active)
   Her thesis hasn't been completed yet by her. (Passive)
4. The boys haven't used the chemicals in the laboratory for some good purpose. (Active)
   The chemicals in the laboratory haven't been used for some good purpose by the boys. (Passive)

(iv) ***Past Indefinite***

1. She ascended the mountain peak just in an hour. (Active)
   The mountain peak was ascended by her just in an hour. (Passive)
2. The abductors held the children tightly. (Active)
   The children were held tightly by the abductors. (Passive)
3. She did not give much problem to her mother while learning to speak. (Active)
   Much problem to her mother was not given by her while learning to speak. (Passive)
4. They did not mend their ways of living. (Active)
   Their ways of living were not mended by them. (Passive)

(v) ***Past Continuous***

1. The girl was practising her speech that she was going to deliver the next week. (Active)
   Her speech that she was going to deliver the next week was being practised by the girl. (Passive)
2. The children were tearing the pages of their books during summer vacation. (Active)
   The pages of their books were being torn by the children during summer vacation. (Passive)
3. The worker was not greasing the bike. (Active)
   The bike was not being greased by the worker. (Passive)
4. The fishermen were not casting the nests. (Active)
   The nests were not being cast by the fishermen. (Passive)

(vi) ***Past Perfect***

1. The boy had rolled the trolley along the fence. (Active)
   The trolley had been rolled along the fence by the boy. (Passive)
2. The girls had translated all the letters into French. (Active)
   All the letters had been translated into French by the girls. (Passive)
3. The manager had not signed the documents. (Active)
   The documents had not been signed by the manager. (Passive)
4. We had not brought the newspaper from the kiosk. (Active)
   The newspaper had not been brought from the kiosk by us. (Passive)

(vii) ***Future Indefinite***

1. Fire will burn his house to a cinder. (Active)
   His house will be burnt to a cinder by fire. (Passive)
2. The government will not allow anybody to cut forests. (Active)
   Nobody will be allowed to cut forests by the government. (Passive)

(viii) ***Future Perfect***

1. India will have realized her vision by 2020. (Active)
   Her vision will have been realized by 2020 by India. **Or** Her vision will have been realized by India by 2020) (Passive)
2. The explorers will have explored an island full of iron ore. (Active)
   An island full of iron ore will have been explored by the explorers. (Passive)

B. Passive Voice of Imperative Sentences

(i) ***Requests***

1. Please turn off the tap.
   You are requested to turn off the tap.
2. Please/ kindly bring me a glass of water.
   You are requested to bring me a glass of water.

(ii) ***Proposals/Suggestions***

Let us have a cup of tea.

It is proposed or suggested that we should have a cup of tea.

(iii) ***Orders/Commands***

Put these pieces of paper in the bin.

You are ordered to put these pieces of paper in the bin.

(iv) ***Prohibition***

Don't pluck flowers.
You are forbidden to pluck flowers.

(v) ***Advice***

Help the needy.
Let the needy be helped. **Or**, You are advised to help the needy.

C. Optative Sentences

1. May you live long!
   It is wished that you should live long.
2. May God bless you!
   It is prayed that God may bless you.
3. O for a glass of water!
   A glass of water is desired at once.

D. Interrogative Sentences

(i) ***When the sentence starts with a primary modal***

1. Do the corals make reefs?
   Are reefs made of corals?
2. Have the frogs laid eggs on the floating leaves of the plants?
   Have the eggs been laid by the frogs on the floating leaves of the plants?
3. Is the flower giving out a pleasant smell?
   Is a pleasant smell being given out by the flower?
4. Are other countries of the world not helping the Ethiopians?
   Are the Ethiopians not being helped by other countries of the world?
5. Did Howard Trevor, (an English actor) play character role of Gandhi well?
   Was character role of Gandhi played well by Howard Trevor (an English actor)?

(ii) ***When the sentence starts with a modal auxiliary***

1. Can the stillness in the air make the day stuffy?
   Can the day be made stuffy by the stillnesss in the air?
2. Will this aardvark eat ants?
   Will ants be eaten by this aardvark?
3. May he contact you soon?
   May you be contacted soon by him?

4. Should I drop a line to him?
   Should a line be dropped to him by me?

(iii) ***When the sentence starts with a 'wh' word (i.e. a Relative Pronoun or a Relative Adverb)***

1. Who is making a paper dustbin?
   By whom is a paper dustbin being made?
2. What was the boy telling his friend?
   What was his friend being told to by the boy? **Or**, what was being told to his friend by the boy?
3. Where does she place her make up kit?
   Where is her make-up kit placed by her?
4. How would you break such a strong lock?
   How would such a strong lock be broken by you?
5. Why have you withdrawn all of your cash?
   Why has all of your cash been withdrawn by you?

E. Passive Voice of Intransitive Verbs

Usually intransitive verbs do not have a passive form but sometimes some intransitive verbs can have their passive forms also.

1. Butter is soft to touch.
   Butter is soft when touched. **Or**, Butter is soft when it is touched.
2. Honey is sweet to taste **Or** honey tastes sweet.
   Honey is sweet when tasted. **Or**, Honey is sweet when it is tasted.

F. Some other methods

(i) ***In the following sentences a preposition other than 'by' is used.***

1. This jug contains juice.
   Juice is contained in this jug.
2. Her conduct surprised me.
   I was surprised at her conduct.
3. The audience thronged the hall.
   The hall was thronged with the audience.

(ii) ***In some sentences bearing a phrase (having a preposition) the preposition is also retained in the passive voice.***

1. The thief broke into the house.
   The house was broken into by the thief.

2. He charged her with murder.
   She was charged with murder (by him).
3. They played upon your weaknesses.
   Your weaknesses were played upon by them.

(iii) ***In the sentences such as those given below, there is no need to use 'by' in the passive voice.***

1. One must do one's duty.
   Duty must be done.
2. The police caught the thief.
   The thief was caught.
3. Somebody wants you in the club.
   You are wanted in the club.

(iv) ***Some sentences have a double object. Such sentences can have two passive voices.***

1. She gave me a new bag.
   A new bag was given to me by her. **Or**, was given a new bag by her.
2. Romeo has written a letter to his father.
   A letter has been written to his father by Romeo. **Or**, His father has been written a letter by Romeo.
3. He passed me the sauce bottle.
   The sauce bottle was passed to me by him. **Or**, I was passed the sauce bottle by him.

(v) ***Infinitives***

1. You have to remove this dust.
   This dust has to be removed by you.
2. It is time to eat lunch.
   It is time for lunch to be eaten.
3. She likes her friends to praise her.
   She likes to be praised by her friends.

Exercise 1

Give Passive Voice of the following.

1. Karina squeezed the toothpaste with all her strength.

 ____

2. Some workers spun wool into the yarn.

 ____

3. My uncle will review this case.

 ____

4. The chef removed the lid over the bowl.

 ____

5. She rowed across the river alone.

 ____

6. Martin has put all the things on the shelf in a good manner.

 ____

7. The defence minister had already proposed a new scheme to control information.

 ____

 ____

8. Time and tide wait for none.

 ____

9. Jack usually dumps his dresses on the bed.

 ____

10. The snow dogs will have dragged the sledge.

 ____

11. The students are reading comics and detective novels.

 ____

12. The monkey was looking for some grains and bananas.

 ____

Exercise 2

Give Passive Voice of the following.

1. What was the lion doing in the jungle?

   ____

2. Why are you taking the matter so seriously?

   ____

3. Whom do you want to see?

   ____

4. Where have you seen the aircraft?

   ____

5. Who buried these bones under the soil?

   ____

6. How did she cross the mountain so easily?

   ____

7. Why will you appoint Mr John as the manager?

   ____

8. Who nabbed the gangsters?

   ____

9. What had he purchased from New Zealand during his trip?

   ____

10. Who will bell the cat?

    ____

Exercise 3

Give the Passive Voice of the following.

1. Work hard.

   ____

2. Have you fared well in your examination?

____

3. Are the boys colouring the pictures?

____

4. Sit down, please.

____

5. Post this letter at once.

____

6. May you live long!

____

7. May you stand first in the class!

____

8. Sugar tastes sweet.

____

9. Silk feels soft to touch.

____

10. The boys laughed at the beggar.

____

11. Jack knocked on the door.

____

12. Did the lioness leave any imprints of her paws?

____

13. Were the mice looking at the piece of cake merrily?

____

14. Let us have some snacks and tea.

____

15. Could I use your pen?

16. May you be prosperous!

17. Her austere simplicity impressed him a lot.

18. Don't move.

19. I know him very well.

20. His behaviour annoyed me.

Exercise 4

Give Active Voice of the following sentences.

1. The radio was turned on by Tina.

2. It is time for the shop to be opened.

3. The book is banged shut by Harry.

4. Some plants are said to be dwarf-trees.

5. The truck is being driven by the driver at a terrific speed.

6. After the blast, the ship was being searched by the sea authorities.

7. Was the wand swished in the air by the fairy?

____

8. Is the aeroplane being flown by a trainee pilot?

____

9. The fly has been trapped by a spider into its web.

____

10. The hedges in the lawn had been given round ends by the gardener.

____

11. The shampoo blended with henna is being sold by a multinational company.

____

12. Has a burnished arrow been flown over the battlefield as a warning by the warrior?

____

13. You are forbidden to touch my books.

____

14. It is suggested that we should sit under the tree.

____

15. You are requested to help me solve this sum.

____

16. Should a message be sent to him?

____

17. Wax is greasy when touched.

____

18. He is known to me.

____

19. Why has this company not been allowed to operate in Singapore?

____

20. Were the dry seeds being broadcast in the fields by the farmers?

____

UNIT 12

DIRECT-INDIRECT SPEECH

A. Reporting verb in the present or future tense

When the Reporting verb is in the present or future tense, there will be no change in the tense of the Indirect Speech.

Examples

1. Neil says to Peter, "the plants are useful to man in many ways." (Direct)
   Neil tells Peter that the plants are useful to man in many ways. (Indirect)
2. Lucky will say to Tina, "I would prefer staying here than going further anymore." (Direct)
   Lucky will tell Tina, that he would prefer staying here than going further anymore. (Indirect)

Exercise 1

Give the Indirect Speech of the following sentences.

1. Harry says, "It rains heavily on the hill-side."

   ____

2. Tina will say, "My mother is cutting vegetables and fruits. We are expecting guests today."

   ____

   ____

3. Jack will say to Peter, "I have seen this boy somewhere before."

   ____

4. Mary says to Lily, "A carpenter is expert in driving the nails properly in wood."

   ____

   ____

5. James says to Mary, “The prince came out with a burnished sword.”

____

6. Maya will say, “You must apply for this post.”

____

7. Kelly says to Simmy, “The gangsters bound her hand and foot.”

____

8. Robert will say to Jacob, “I want to buy these lightweight sunglasses.”

____

Exercise 2

Give Direct Speech of the following sentences.

1. Sam tells Victor that the trees in the forest are being cut by the smugglers and are being sold to the foreigners at high prices.

____

____

2. Barry says that his uncle, being a member of the crew, often keeps sailing through the seas.

____

____

3. Tony says that the golden rays of the sun fall on the fluffy clouds in a beautiful pattern.

____

____

4. David tells James that he has no time to see his own weaknesses.

____

5. Sophia tells Annie that she will shoot an angular goal in the final match and will become victorious.

____

____

6. The child tells his mother that he has drunk half a glass of milk and the rest of the milk he will take after playing with his friend.

____

____

7. The boy tells his friends that the elephant gave a yank to the berry tree and soon after, it snapped in two.

____

____

8. The girl tells her aunt that whenever she tried to walk over the marble floor, she had a fall for its being so slippery.

____

____

9. He says that his brother will explore the forest on foot.

____

10. The servant tells the master that he could not work properly yesterday because he was not feeling well.

____

____

B. Reporting Verb in the past tense (Direct Speech in present tense)

When the Reporting Verb is in the past tense the words showing nearness in time and place are changed into words expressing distance.

here	there
now	then
ago	before
this	that
these	those
today	that day
yesterday	the previous day
tomorrow	the next day
thus	so
last night/ week/ month/ year	the previous night/ week/ month/ year

Affirmative Sentences

1. Harry said to Bobby, "My brother types letters on a typewriter but I work on a computer."
   Harry told Bobby that his brother typed letters on a typewriter but he worked on a computer.

2. Rita said to Julie, "I am working as an editor in a big publishing house."
   Rita told Julie that she was working as an editor in a big publishing house.

3. Julie said to Rita, "I have sketched a few cartoons."
   Julie told Rita that she had sketched a few cartoons.

4. John said to Tony, "I do not like you to poke your nose into my affairs."
   John told Tony that he did not like him to poke his nose into his affairs.

Exercise 3

Give the Indirect Speech of the following.

1. Harry said to Parker, "Daisy has just qualified as a doctor."

   ____

2. Tina said to Ruby, "John has been rebuked for making a noise."

   ____

   ____

3. Miley said to Julie, "We are getting our house rebuilt."

   ____

   ____

4. Henry said to Robin, "The police often recover a large number of stolen articles from the gangs of robbers."

   ____

   ____

5. Lily said to Maya, "The manager has recorded your statement."

   ____

   ____

6. Mr Gower said to his secretary, "You are not working on this topic in a proper manner."

7. John said to Martin, "I am happy that you still hold fast to this principle."

8. Max said to Alex, "You do not know how to make a good job of it."

9. Tony said to Paul, "It is good if you clamp this plank to the edge of this table."

10. John said to Lily, "You haven't even finished your work yet."

Exercise 4

Give the Direct Speech of the following sentences.

1. The tailor told the actor that a sea green nightgown looked good on him.

2. The girl told her mother that she had definitely made up her deficiency in studies then.

3. The private detective told the policeman that he had seen the thief running but he took him for an innocent man and let him run away.

4. Sam told John that the sale of readymade garments was going to be a lucrative one because some of the foreign companies had shown great interest in the Indian garments.

____

____

____

5. The old man told us that a big cache of arms had been seized by the local police.

____

____

6. The businessman told the share holders that the company had decided to increase the production of nylon fibre and for that it was going to raise funds.

____

____

7. The scientist told the science students that ever since the plants have appeared on the earth they have been serving mankind without demur.

____

____

8. The boy said that he had already seen the eruption of the volcano when he was working in a hilly earthquake prone region of the country.

____

____

9. The hunter told the boy that he hadn't ever killed a forest animal but he had trapped a few whom he had sold to the master of a circus.

____

____

10. The old lady told the press reporter that the boat she was sailing in had once capsized all of a sudden.

____

____

C. Reporting Verb in the past tense (Direct Speech in the past tense)

Note the changes in the indirect speech of the following sentences in direct speech.

Direct Speech

1. Karina said to Emily, "You danced extremely well."
2. Honey said to Tony, "Kelly was putting on a light make-up."
3. Dolly said to Alex, "My uncle did not want anybody to talk to him in a sad mood."
4. John said to Parker, "My aunt was not going to give up her pride in her ancestry at any cost."

Indirect Speech

1. Karina told Emily that she had danced extremely well.
2. Honey told Tony that Kelly had been putting on a light make-up.
3. Dolly told Alex that her uncle had not wanted anybody to talk to him in a sad mood.
4. John told Parker that his aunt had not been going to give up her pride in her ancestry at any cost.

Note : In sentences No. 3 and 4 above, if the past indefinite and past continuous tenses respectively are not changed into past perfect and past perfect continuous tenses, the sentences will still be considered correct, as they also contain habitual truth.

Exercise 5

Give Indirect Speech of the following.

1. Robert said to Kelvin, "I crossed the bridge within a few minutes."

   ____

2. Shelly said to Rosy, "The boys were holding bouquets of flowers while the girls were giving them instructions."

   ____

   ____

3. Harry said to John, "They had already arranged a military band to make the celebrations a memorable event."

   ____

   ____

4. Lucy said to Daizy, "My brother's friend did not wish to leave Singapore."

   ____

5. Juliet said to Rose, "The food was not good and the drinks were not up to mark either in the party."

____

____

6. Jack said to Mr Ford, "I did not say anything about the bad arrangement of lighting inside the hall."

____

____

7. The officer said to the farmers, "Last year heavy rains affected the crops badly."

____

____

8. The manager said to the head chef, "Your subordinates were not cooking good dishes."

____

____

9. Peter said to Martin, "Your friends were drawing a cart when I went to see them."

____

____

10. Jane said to Mary, "My brother did not know how to drive a steamer."

____

____

Exercise 6

Give the Direct Speech of the following.

1. Julia told Tina that she had made a heavy purchase at the sales counter in the City Garments the previous day.

____

____

2. The fisherman told me that once he had been looking for a big catch at sea when a giant fish crashed into his boat.

____

____

3. The chef told the waiter that he had put the kettle on the stove and was then waiting for tea to boil.

____

____

4. The soldier told his friends that he had seen a terrorist crawling out of a hideout.

____

____

5. The child told the teacher that she had coloured all the pictures with crayons.

____

6. The nurse told the patient's friend that the patient had been allowed to amble about in the lawn for an hour.

____

____

7. Lily told Karina that she had been brushing her hair when a cold gale ruffled it.

____

____

8. The hunter told the boys that the horseman had whipped the horse to gallop.

____

9. My aunt told me that she hadn't ever liked the children weeping for chocolates and toffees.

____

____

10. The botanist told the fruitseller that the apples on the trees were being injected with newly invented drugs to increase their sizes.

____

____

D. Reporting Verb in the past tense (Direct speech in the future tense)

Shall *and* ***will*** *should be changed into* ***would***

Examples

1. The chief said to the crew, "The ship Titanic will lie off the ship Neil."
   The chief told the crew that the ship Titanic would lie off the ship Neil.
2. The head clerk said, "I will have gone through the file once again by then."
   The head clerk said that he would have gone through the file once again by then.

Exercise 7

Give Indirect Speech of the following.

1. Tony said to Riya, "The big diamond will have been cut by them."

   ____

2. Gomes said to Simmy, "I won't purchase a lidless dustbin."

   ____

3. Danny said to Max, "The cat will be licking her injured paw."

   ____

4. Julie said to Mary, "You will get tangy snacks and other eatables at the school tuck-shop."

   ____

5. The mother said to the child, "You will not keep anything back from me."

   ____

6. The coach said to the players, "Just one sip of this tonic will boost up your drooping spirits."

   ____

7. The gatekeeper said to the boy, "You will be informed soon about it."

   ____

8. The shopkeeper said to the customer, "I won't exchange this old chair for a new one."

9. The boy said to his friend, "Tomorrow my uncle will be given a green signal to go abroad."

10. John said to Peter, "You won't be allowed to keep all the coins with yourself."

Exercise 8

Give the Direct Speech of the following sentences.

1. My aunt told to my mother that her son would have learned manners by then.

2. My brother told my sister that she would be getting her hair curled when the guests appeared.

3. Henry told Charles that he would definitely fight for the rights of the poor people.

4. Tina told her brother that she would have definitely completed her thesis by the end of that month.

5. Rosy told Timmy that her brother would take part in the Olympics the next year.

6. The student told the teacher that he would work hard and win the scholarship.

____

7. Lolita told Ruby that her mother would fall a victim to influenza because she was still strolling in the lawn when the evening had turned so bitterly cold.

____

____

8. My uncle told us that the cubs would cling together as the night got colder.

____

9. The old woman told the investigator that she would see the robber through the glass window.

____

____

10. The old man told the optician that he would not spend much on the glasses because he was not going to be helped by them in any way for his being blind.

____

____

E. Reporting Verb in Past Tense (Imperative Sentences)

1. Ajay said to Joe, "Don't disturb me."
   Ajay forbade Joe to disturb him.

2. Sophia said to Annie, "Let us sit under the tree."
   Sophia proposed to Annie to sit under the tree.

   Or

   Sophia proposed (or suggested) to Annie that they should sit under the tree.

3. Tina said to Ruby, "Please post this letter."
   Tina requested Ruby to post that letter.

4. Zenith said to Rayan, "Have some juice."
   Zenith offered Rayan some juice.

5. The teacher said to the peon, "Bring me some chalk at once."
   The teacher ordered the peon to bring him some chalk at once.

Exercise 9

Give the Indirect Speech of the following sentences.

1. Alex said to Martin, "Work hard."

   ____

2. James said to Maya, "Please give me a glass of water."

   ____

3. Lily said to Peter, "Don't move."

   ____

4. Adam said to Harry, "Let us have a cup of tea."

   ____

5. John said to Mary, "Have some snacks."

   ____

6. Mendis said to Feroz, "Listen to me please."

   ____

7. Mr Simon said to Mr David, "Let us have some walk."

   ____

8. Tina said to Rosy, "Don't disturb me."

   ____

9. Harry said to Lily, "Please wait for me."

   ____

10. Max said to Ford, "Stop here."

    ____

Exercise 10

Give the Direct Speech of the following sentences:

1. Julie advised her sister that she should learn various arts to succeed in life.

   ____

2. John proposed to his friends to have a short walk daily.

3. The teacher ordered the student to stand up on the bench.

4. My friend requested me to buy him a new pen from the main market.

5. The gardener forbade the children to play in the garden.

6. Mr Hood offered Mr David some snacks.

7. My aunt advised me to get up with the first ray of the sun and take some exercise to keep fresh both body and mind.

8. I requested my friend to bring me some poster, colours and brushes from the nearby shop.

9. My friend, shivering with cold, suggested that we should sit around a roaring fire and have a scalding hot coffee.

10. The police officer advised the prisoner not to do anything wrong in future.

F. Reporting Verb in past tense (Exclamatory Sentences)

1. The boy said, "What a lovely star it is!"
   The boy exclaimed with joy that it was a very lovely star.
2. The child said, "How beautiful the rainbow is!"
   The child exclaimed with joy that the rainbow was very beautiful.
3. The girl said, "What an ugly bird it is!"
   The girl exclaimed with contempt that the bird was very ugly.
4. The old man said, "May God bless you!"
   The old man wished that God might bless me.
5. The old woman said to the king, "May you be ruined!"
   The old woman cursed the king wishing (or praying) that he might be ruined.

Exercise 11

Give the Indirect Speech of the following sentences.

1. The old man said, "May you live long!"

   ____

2. The old woman said, "May you fail in your mission!"

   ____

3. The old woman said, "May you prosper!"

   ____

4. The girl said, "What a beautiful snail it is!"

   ____

5. The boy said, "How beautiful the crown is!"

   ____

6. The old man said, "May you become rich!"

   ____

7. The child said, "What a huge animal it is!"

   ____

8. The girl said, "What a foul smell this oil gives!"

9. My grandmother said, "May you get succeed in your enterprise!"

10. My uncle said, "How strange this bird is!"

Exercise 12

Give the Direct Speech of the following sentences.

1. The old woman wished that I might be victorious in my venture.

2. The old man cursed the king wishing that he might lose all his wealth as well as fame.

3. The child exclaimed with joy that the stars looked very beautiful.

4. The girl exclaimed with surprise that the aeroplane was looking like a bird.

5. The girl exclaimed with contempt that the wild beast was very ugly.

6. The woman exclaimed with joy that her husband had trimmed down to 70 kg in just two months.

7. The beggar prayed that mankind might live in peace.

8. The old man wished that man might be provided with wisdom.

9. The child exclaimed with joy that the painting was really very beautiful.

____

10. The old woman cursed the naughty boy wishing that he might fail in the examination.

____

G. Interrogative sentences starting with modals or primary modals

1. Marco said to Lily, "Can you make an Italian dish?"
   Marco asked Lily if she could make an Italian dish.
2. Robert said to Danny, "Would you like to accompany me?"
   Robert asked Danny if he would like to accompany him.
3. Tina said to Ruby, "Should I open the windows?"
   Tina asked Ruby if she should open the windows.

Exercise 13

Give Indirect Speech of the following.

1. John said to Tony, "Should I hire a taxi for you?"

____

2. Robin said to Bobby, "Will you apply oil to your new motorbike?"

____

3. Paul said to Twinkle, "Can you drive the car through this muddy street?"

____

4. Daisy said to Lily, "Would you like to dance with me?"

____

5. Sophia said to Maria, "Have you decided to emigrate to England?"

____

6. Tina said to Peter, "Are you ready to help me?"

____

7. Alice said to Lolita, "Do you know the exact meaning of this word?"

____

8. Henry said to Max, "Did your brother sail the boat across the river?"

9. Adam said to Peter, "Is your sister learning martial arts these days?"

10. Mr Paul said to Mr David, "Do you understand the language of birds?"

11. The lawyer said to the culprit, "Have you really misappropriated the funds of the trust?"

12. The woodcutter said to the god Mercury, "Can't you make the people learn the value of flora and fauna?"

13. The boy said to his friend, "Don't you get hold of such a simple idea?"

14. The girl said to her uncle, "Had the army set off on the campaign Sarpnash?"

15. The teacher said to the student, "Are there any questions excessively tough?"

Exercise 14

Give Direct Speech of the following sentence.

1. Lucy asked Jane if she could count the snail shells lying on the beach.

2. Tina asked Sara if she had boiled the eggs for the guests.

3. Jack asked Adam if he would affix the stamps to the top of the letters for him.

4. Dolly asked Rose if her father was working as a manager in a five star hotel.

5. Sunny asked Daizy if she had applied for the job of a navy officer.

6. The shopkeeper asked the customer if he would like to see some more exotic pairs of shoes.

7. The child asked her mother if there was some more fresh cheese in the tray.

8. The old man asked his son if he could use his motorbike.

9. The wife asked her husband if he would allow her to purchase some dresses from the sales counter.

10. The boy asked the shopkeeper if he could cut off a length of wire from the coil.

H. Interrogative sentences starting with wh– words

1. The doctor said to the patient, "What did you eat at the hotel yesterday?"
   The doctor asked the patient what he had taken at the hotel the previous day.
2. The man said to the taxidermist, "Why haven't you done the filling of straw in the skin of the leopard?"
   The man demeaned of the taxidermist why he hadn't done the filling of straw in the skin of leopard.
3. The mother said to her daughter, "Where did you buy this tawdry jewellery from?"
   The mother asked her daughter where she had bought that tawdry jewellery from.

Exercise 15

Give the Indirect Speech of the following sentences.

1. The customer said to the shopkeeper, "When should I come again to you for table knives, forks and burnished spoons?"

   ____

   ____

2. The husband said to his wife, "Why are you boiling with rage?"

   ____

3. The conductor said to the passenger, "Why haven't you purchased the ticket?"

   ____

   ____

4. The mother said to the son, "When will you have finished your homework?"

   ____

   ____

5. Karina said to Joe, "Where have you put your wallet?"

   ____

6. The mother said to the daughter, "Why don't you do such chores by yourself?"

   ____

   ____

7. Nancy said to Ruby, "How fast did the waiter serve us meal?"

____

8. Lily said to John, "Why are you apprehensive of the future?"

____

9. The businessman said to the sea-men, "Why have you released my vessel into the sea now?"

____

____

10. The cowboy said to the officer, "When should I go to the hillside to bring back the cattle?"

____

____

Exercise 16

Give Direct Speech of the following sentences.

1. The child asked his mother when he should ask for chocolates and toffees.

____

____

2. The cobbler asked the customer why he wanted his boots to be given stitching along the back part.

____

____

3. The officer asked the car driver from where he had bought that wheelclamp.

____

____

4. Maria asked Julie how she had managed to make good her escape.

____

____

5. David asked Robert when he had had a close shave with a tiger.

____

____

6. The officer asked the driver what made him stop the lorry well before the traffic lights.

____

____

7. The teacher asked the student why he had created a disturbance in the class.

____

____

8. The instructor asked the student why he had not allowed the solution to come to boil when he had been instructed for that.

____

____

9. The doctor asked the patient who had allowed him to move about on crutches.

____

____

10. The soldier asked the prisoner when he would divulge the identity of his companions.

____

____

UNIT 13

PHRASES

1. Adjective Phrases

Read the following sentences.

Andrew was an **intelligent** boy. (Adjective)
Andrew was a boy **full of intelligence**. (Adjective Phrase)

An ***adjective phrase*** *can usually be used in place of an* ***adjective***.

Exercise 1

Underline the Adjective Phrases and circle the Adjectives in each of the following sentences.

1. Tina wore a shirt made of cotton.
2. She folded out the big map.
3. The sky was crowded with the kites of different colours.
4. He sailed in a boat of teak wood.
5. She is a poetess of gloomy poems.
6. You need a true and honest friend.
7. He pushed away the box full of antiques.
8. He was in a black mood.
9. He shot me a black look.
10. The poor old beggar bedded down on the stack of straw.
11. He seems to be in a bad temper.
12. The rosy light of the sun spread over the whole area.
13. The cruel hunter gunned down a brace of birds of a rare species.

14. The old motorbike had a jerky start.

15. That was a colourful stone of a big size.

Exercise 2

In the following sentences, replace the Adjectives by Adjective Phrases.

1. Mr Alex bought a new green cycle while his brother bought an old motorbike.

____

____

2. His courageous deed made him a hero among the public in a day.

____

3. Her books lay scattered over the marble floor.

____

4. Lily could not remember where she had left her gold ring.

____

5. Tears trickled down her dry cheeks.

____

6. The raindrops dashed against the wooden planks around the field.

____

7. The buff paper of the book looks rusty.

____

8. The lump of copper was beaten out into long wires.

____

9. She became an acclaimed painter as she painted some unmatchable pictures on the canvas.

____

____

10. She could not make much progress in life for she was an insincere woman.

____

____

11. The boat sailed ahead on the blue surface of the sea.

____

12. He played extremely well in the match yet he could not register his first win over the Swedish player.

____

____

13. In spite of his best efforts he could not win a leading position in his party.

____

____

14. Last night a gang of robbers broke into my neighbour's house.

____

____

15. The young boy gave a polish to his shabby shoes.

____

2. Adverb Phrases

Read the following sentences.

1. (a) He fought **bravely**. (Adverb showing how i.e. manner)
   (b) He fought **with great bravery**. (Phrase showing how i.e. manner)

2. (a) They are taking tea **now**. (Adverb showing when i.e. time)
   (b) They are taking tea **at the moment**. (Phrase showing when i.e. time)

3. (a) The bullet hit him **here**. (Adverb showing where i.e. place)
   (b) The bullet hit him **on this spot**. (Phrase showing where i.e. place)

*Usually an **adverb phrase** can be used in place of an **adverb**.*

Exercise 3

Underline the Adverb Phrase and circle the Adverb, if any, in each of the following sentences.

1. She held her breath and walked up to the exit slowly.

2. The batsman struck the ball wonderfully and it raced down out of fence for four.
3. My brother found a magic stone from this place.
4. We may get the bus for Delhi from there.
5. The habit of telling lies affected his reputation adversely.
6. Even if he was strong and learned he could not make progress remarkably.
7. As soon as he heard the news, he came to me straightaway.
8. The hotel was buzzing at the time in the day and I too could hear the sound of steps being put heavily on the wooden plank.
9. The lorry that was blown apart, was being driven by a young man who was known for his matchless acuity in driving vehicles accurately.
10. The tight shoe brought about a blister on the toe of my foot.
11. She corked in bottle tightly.
12. Make yourself at home.
13. The western fashion is assimilating into the Indian culture at an alarming speed.
14. She spoke to him at the top of her voice.
15. The little girl writes a letter to her mother in a neat hand.

Exercise 4

Replace Adverbs in the following sentences by appropriate Adverb Phrases.

1. Mr Smith was formerly the president of this club.

   ____

2. Before leaving the place Tina informed her friend that she would come back soon.

   ____

   ____

3. A gull flew away swiftly.

   ____

4. A horror novel has recently been launched in America.

   ____

5. Though Jack could not find his own watch, he cheerfully accepted another one in lieu of it.

6. A tall boy stepped out of the house cautiously.

7. Her mother spoke to her daughter softly as she wanted to instil in her mind the real value of studies.

8. The old feeble pale man fell down heavily on the dock of the ship.

9. The burnished arrow came zooming and struck in the wooden door deeply.

10. He laughed angrily.

11. The maid handled the crockery clumsily.

12. Miss Mary talked to her brother rudely.

13. The child lost his eraser somewhere here.

14. She knocked on the door loudly.

15. The four troops stepped forward.

---

3. Noun Phrases

Read the following sentences.

He likes **butter**. (Noun)
He likes **to eat butter**. (Noun Phrase)

*Usually a **noun phrase** can be used in place of a **noun**.*

Exercise 5

Underline the Noun Phrase in each of the following sentences.

1. It is bad to make fun of others.
2. He loves to tease the birds and animals.
3. My brother did not bother to reach the hall on time.
4. The boy refused to type the letter.
5. John trapped a brace of pigeons.
6. Dancing on the marble floor is not easy.
7. Cutting grass on a hot summer day is not advisable.
8. To drive on this road slowly is not allowed.
9. She promised to meet me again.
10. She denies having stolen my watch.
11. My brother wished to see the brave boys who had saved the lives of many drowning children.
12. She refused to answer my question.
13. To sing loudly is not a sign of intelligence.
14. Have you thought about going abroad?
15. To win the first prize was the heart's desire of Tony.

UNIT 14

THE CLAUSE

A Clause has a subject and a finite verb, but still it does not make a complete sense on its own.

(i) She is the girl <u>who has made her mark as a dancer</u>.
(ii) We'll go to the beach at the time <u>when there is no rain</u>.

Underlined words are Clauses.

Classification of CLAUSES

Clauses can be classified in the following way.

I. Adjective Clause
II. Adverb Clause
III Noun Clause

I Adjective clause

An Adjective Clause does the function of an Adjective. Usually an *adjective phrase* can be replaced by an *adjective clause*.

Examples

A mastiff is a dog **with strong jaws.** (Phrase)
A mastiff is a dog **which has strong jaws.** (Clause)

Exercise 1

Replace each of the following Phrases by an Adjective Clause.

1. He was bitten off by a <u>dog of black colour</u>.

____

2. A lion <u>with a long mane</u> was caught by the hunter.

____

3. The shark with a <u>dorsal fin of broad width</u> swam fast.

____

4. The elephant with a big trunk was allowed to stroll along the hillside.

____

5. The plants with thick leaves full of thorns grow in deserts.

____

6. The book with illustrated pages is read by my brother.

____

7. The bell of a burnished metal rang sweetly.

____

8. The gardener hacked off the leaves of brown colour.

____

9. A man of a strong physique was found dead on the edge of the river.

____

10. The tree with blade like leaves was cut down by the cruel woodcutter.

____

II Adverb Clauses

Read the following sentences.

(i) She found a coin **at this place**.
She found a coin **where I had guessed**.

(ii) She ran **at a great speed**.
Her speed was great **while she ran**.

Exercise 2

Replace each of the following Adverb Phrases by an Adverb Clause of the same meaning.

1. The workers have given a call for strike from this very moment.

____

2. We accepted the deal without hesitation.

____

3. The truck ran at a terrible speed.

____

4. I found a ring at this place.

____

5. He replied with perfect honesty.

____

6. She opened the door in a quick manner.

____

7. She is in Russia at the moment.

____

8. The boy cried in a loud voice.

____

9. The horse accepted husk of grams in a cheerful mood.

____

10. She is expecting guests in the evening.

____

III Noun Clause

Read the following sentences.

He requested me **to attend the class.**
He requested me that **I should attend the class.**

Exercise 3

Replace each of the following Adverb Phrases by a Noun Clause of the same meaning.

1. She wanted to eat oranges.

____

2. He decided to stay at home.

____

3. The officer ordered the clerk <u>to leave the room at once</u>.

____

4. Maria proposed to us <u>to have a cup of tea</u>.

____

5. The clerk requested the officer <u>to grant him leave for two days</u>.

____

6. I advised him <u>to work hard</u>.

____

7. He was allowed <u>to carry on his business</u>.

____

8. She was anxious <u>to top the list of successful candidates</u>.

____

9. The teacher ordered the peon <u>to bring the file</u>.

____

10. We decided <u>to live in India forever</u>.

____

UNIT 15

RELATIVE ADVERBS

When, where, why, how *are commonly used Relative Adverbs.*

Examples

1. Sunday is the day **when** I go to a hotel for dinner.
2. Delhi is the city **where** I spent the prime of my life.
3. The reason **why** he does not care for you is that he is a man of a malicious nature.
4. He explained to me the way **how** he could accumulate so much wealth.

Exercise 1

Fill in the blanks with 'when', 'how', 'why' or 'where' as Relative Adverbs.

1. This is the road ___________ I found a gold coin.
2. I do not know the reason ___________ he dislikes you.
3. She informed me the time ___________ she would make good her escape from the prison.
4. Monday is the day ___________ I go to the hospital to serve the needy.
5. This is the village ___________ I often came to see the fair.
6. The reason ___________ he does not brush his teeth is that he has lost all of his teeth except one.
7. The reason ___________ the clouds are scudding across the sky is that the wind is pushing them hard.
8. I do not understand the method ___________ he will manage to collect the funds for this humanitarian project.
9. We do not know the time ___________ he gets up in the morning.
10. This is the room ___________ the bullet-ridden body of a soldier was found.
11. All of us know very well the reason ___________ the blades of grass are waving.
12. Africa is the continent ___________ flora and fauna is found in abundance.

Exercise 2

Join each of the following pairs of sentences/clauses with 'when', 'where', 'how', 'why' as Relative Adverbs. The first one has been done for you.

1. (a) None of us knows the time.
   (b) It will snow some time.
   None of us knows the time when it will snow.

2. (a) The reason is still not known to anybody.
   (b) He loves his sister so much.

   ____

3. (a) You should learn.
   (b) There is a method of solving these sums.

   ____

4. (a) Canada is the country.
   (b) The apples of good quality are found there.

   ____

5. (a) Everybody was surprised/ amazed at the way.
   (b) He managed to save the drowning child.

   ____

6. (a) You should try to understand the reason.
   (b) He beat your dog so mercilessly.

   ____

7. (a) Sunday is the day.
   (b) I go to the beach.

   ____

8. (a) The police have learned the tactics.
   (b) Now they can catch the thieves without delay.

   ____

9. (a) These are the museums.
   (b) You can see the pastels and models of skeletons of the dinosaurs there.

   ____

10. (a) Nobody knows the reason.
    (b) Paul does not like his studies.

   ____

UNIT 16

RELATIVE PRONOUNS

The most commonly used Relative Pronouns are **who, whose, whom, that, which and such. . . .as**.

Examples

1. The boy **who** met us in the theatre is a good player of cricket.
2. The girl **whose** father is a doctor lives on the bank of a river.
3. The bird **that** you saw flying was actually a sea-bird.
4. The book **which** you gave me was full of colourful cartoons.
5. The birds **that** flew over the green fields there had come from some other country.
6. These books are not **such as** we read in the library.
7. She is **such** a girl **as** I adore.

Exercise 1

Fill in the blanks with 'who', 'whose', 'whom', 'which', 'that' or 'such as'.

1. He ________ was not much of a wrestler wanted to fight with the world champion.
2. The dog ________ you saw running towards the outskirts was mad.
3. The pen ________ has a burnished steel nib is very expensive.
4. The herd of elephants ________ ran through the forest has been trapped by the hunters.
5. My uncle likes the boy ________ John.
6. He is ________ a boy ________ everybody feels happy to meet.
7. The pieces of paper ________ have been dumped into the dustbin are actually important documents.
8. The island ________ you visited last year has now been devastated by the cyclones.
9. The blue whale ________ was caught by the fisherman was put back into the sea to swim freely.
10. The woodcutter ________ was asked to buy a new axe had not got the money enough for the purpose.

11. The girl ________ uncle was an officer in the army, was not allowed to make her speech.

12. The gate ________ has recently been painted is actually a very old one and it has a great historical importance.

13. The boy ________ dived into the sea could not reach the seashore again.

14. The children ________ were getting ready for Christmas celebrations were wearing colourful dresses.

15. The trees ________ were growing close to one another were not very tall.

Exercise 2

Join the following pairs of sentences with 'who', 'whose', 'whom', 'which' or 'that'. The first one has been done for you.

1. (a) The boy is my benchmate.
   (b) The boy's father is an ambassador.
   The boy whose father is an ambassador is my bench mate.

2. (a) I like the plants.
   (b) Its flowers give out a sweet smell.

   ____

3. (a) My uncle likes the garden.
   (b) The garden is ablaze with violet blossoms.

   ____

4. (a) Kelly likes the birds.
   (b) The birds sing melodious songs.

   ____

5. (a) The dog was as strong as a tiger.
   (b) The dog bit at the thief's hand last night.

   ____

6. (a) The fisherman wanted to catch the fish.
   (b) The fish jumped over the surface of water and again came back spinning in the air.

   ____

7. (a) The farmer ploughed the fields.
   (b) The fields were dry and cracked.

   ____

8. (a) The student was punished by the teacher.
   (b) The student was making faces at the teacher.

____

9. (a) Tina brushed the hair of her doll.
   (b) The doll was gifted by Riya's aunt.

____

10. (a) The cat scratched at the door.
    (b) The door was closed.

____

Compound Relative Pronouns

The commonly used Compound Relative Pronouns are **whoever, whichever** and **whatever**.

Examples

1. **Whichever** of you solves this sum, will be given a prize.
2. Of these five bags, you may take **whichever** you choose.
3. You should do **whatever** you have decided.
4. **Whoever** among you sings a song, will be provided with this trophy.

Exercise 3

Fill in the blanks with 'whichever', 'whoever', 'whatever'.

1. Here are three toys, choose ______________ you like best.
2. ______________ is hidden behind the bush, should come out fast.
3. We'll support ______________ stands for election from our town.
4. ______________ looks attractive should be kept in museum.
5. ______________ is longing for tea should follow me to the dinner room.
6. ______________ deems himself an adroit mechanic should have the acumen to bring this machine back to normal functioning.
7. ______________ tries hard can get success.
8. As regards your terms, we are ready to accept ______________ you offer us.
9. They do not like anything of this house ______________ it may be.
10. I' have found a gold ring. ______________ claims it should contact me on 98130671851.

UNIT 17

COMBINATION OF SENTENCES

I. COMBINATION OF TWO SIMPLE SENTENCES INTO ONE SIMPLE SENTENCE

1. *By using a Noun or Phrase in Apposition*

(a) Shah Jahan built the Taj Mahal.
(b) He was a rich king.
(a+b) Shah Jahan, **a rich king**, built the Taj Mahal.

2. *By using an Infinitive*

(a) He is weak.
(b) He cannot walk.
(a+b) He is too weak **to walk**.

3. *By using a Preposition*

(a) The sun set.
(b) His uncle did not come.
(a+b) His uncle did not come **before** sunset. **Or**,
His uncle did not come even **after** sunset.

4. *By using a Absolute Phrase*

(a) The boy broke the bookshelf in the library.
(b) He was punished.
(a+b) The boy **having broken the bookshelf** in the library was punished.

5. *By using Present Participle*

(a) He was thinking of the death of his father.
(b) He felt sad.
(a+b) **Thinking** of the death of his father, he felt sad.

6. *By using a Perfect Participle*

(a) She had finished knitting.
(b) She went into the computer room.
(a+b) **Having finished** knitting she went into the computer room.

7. *By using Past Participle*

(a) He was defeated by the enemy.
(b) He decided to commit suicide.
(a+ b) **Defeated** by the enemy he decided to commit suicide.

8. *By using an Adverb Phrase/Adverb*

(a) She got up early in the morning.
(b) It was her general routine.
(a+ b) She **often** got up early in the morning.

Exercise 1

Combine each of the following pairs of sentences into one simple sentence.

1 (a) It was very cold.
(b) No one could go outside.

____

2. (a) She tried hard to get at the bunch of grapes.
(b) Her efforts proved useless.

____

____

3. (a) Avogadro was a chemist.
(b) He was an Italian.

____

4. (a) Peter had finished levelling the ground in the lawn.
(b) He went out of the house to see his friends.

____

____

5. (a) The sun rose.
(b) No one in Mr John's house had got up.

____

6. (a) He went to see the movie.
(b) He went there every weekend.

____

7. (a) He was deceived by his rival.
   (b) He decided to leave his country.

____

8. (a) He was tired.
   (b) He wanted some rest.

____

9. (a) The hunter killed some innocent animals.
   (b) He sat down to smoke.

____

____

10. (a) Mr Ford drinks a cup of tea.
    (b) He daily drinks it in the morning.

____

____

11. (a) Shakespeare was a famous dramatist.
    (b) He wrote Macbeth and Othello.

____

____

12. (a) Glasgow is a city in Scotland.
    (b) It is an important commercial centre.

____

13. (a) The thief broke into the house.
    (b) He stole all the valuables from there.

____

____

14. (a) He is dull.
    (b) He does not understand his lessons.

____

15. (a) The book was heavy.
    (b) The child could not carry it to school.

____

II. COMBINATION OF TWO SIMPLE SENTENCES INTO ONE COMPOUND SENTENCE

In each case a coordinating conjunction is used.

yet	but	and	or
otherwise	still	as well as	either... or
neither...nor	not only...but also	both...and	so

Examples

1. (a) He speaks French well.
   (b) He speaks English well.
   He speaks French **and** English well.
   Or
   He speaks **both** French **and** English well.
   Or
   Not only does he speak French **but also** English well.

2. (a) He is rich.
   (b) He is miserly.
   He is rich **but** miserly.

3. (a) He looks healthy.
   (b) He does nothing.
   He looks healthy, **still** he does nothing.

4. (a) The weather was bad.
   (b) We could make it to the shopping complex.
   The weather was bad, **yet** we could make it to the shopping complex.

5. (a) Mary was not willing to meet Mr Henry.
   (b) John was not willing to meet Mr Henry.
   Neither Mary **nor** John was willing to meet Mr Henry.

6. (a) Sing sweetly.
   (b) You won't be given a prize.
   Sing sweetly, **or/otherwise** you won't be given a prize.

7. (a) Play with me.
   (b) Leave this place at once.
   Either play with me **or** leave this place at once.

8. (a) He was exhausted.
   (b) He lay down to rest.
   He was exhausted, **so** he lay down to rest.

Exercise 2

Combine each of the following pairs of sentences into one Compound Sentence.

1. (a) She is tall.
   (b) She is thin.

   ____

2. (a) He is good at sports.
   (b) He is good at studies.

   ____

   ____

3. (a) Dance with us.
   (b) You should go out of the hall.

   ____

   ____

4. (a) Don't go close to that dog.
   (b) It may bite you in the leg.

   ____

   ____

5. (a) Harry was not ready to purchase the bag.
   (b) Sheila was not ready to purchase the bag.

   ____

   ____

6. (a) She was tired.
   (b) She sat down under the tree.

   ____

   ____

7. (a) Mrs James is slim.
   (b) Mrs James is active.

   ____

   ____

8. (a) It was severely cold.
   (b) I switched on the room-heater.

____

____

9. (a) The tree stood bolt upright.
   (b) The boy climbed it.

____

____

10. (a) Twinkle can write German correctly.
    (b) Twinkle can write English correctly.

____

____

11. (a) He has attended many periods in the institute to learn spoken English.
    (b) He cannot speak English fluently.

____

____

12. (a) Don't be in a hurry.
    (b) You may forget to carry some important documents.

____

____

13. (a) She cannot sing well.
    (b) She cannot dance well.

____

14. (a) His mother cooks tasty dishes.
    (b) His sister cooks tasty dishes.

____

____

15. (a) Timmy daily gets up early in the morning.
    (b) He goes out for a short walk.

____

____

III. Combination of Two Simple Sentences into One Complex Sentence

All subordinating conjunctions, relative pronouns and relative adverbs are used to form Complex Sentences.

that	because	when	since	as	although/though
while	until/till	if	whose	whom	provided that
who	which	where	so that	whether	as soon as

Examples

I. By using adjective clause

1. (a) The boy won the first prize in golf.
   (b) He is my classmate.
   (a+b) The boy, who won the first prize in golf, is my classmate.

2. (a) You gave me an umbrella.
   (b) It was full of holes.
   (a+b) The umbrella, which you gave me, was full of holes.

3. (a) The horses were grazing along the forest.
   (b) They were killed by the lion.
   (a+b) The horses which were grazing along the forest were killed by the lion.

4. (a) The boy ascended Mount Everest.
   (b) His father is an engineer.
   (a+b) The boy whose father is an engineer ascended Mount Everest.

5. (a) You saw the bird flying to the east.
   (b) It was an albatross, a sea bird.
   (a+b) The bird which you saw flying to the east was an albatross, a sea bird.

II. By using noun clause

1. (a) He is an innocent boy.
   (b) We all know this.
   (a+b) We all know that he is an innocent boy.

2. (a) Tell me.
   (b) Where has he gone?
   (a+b) Tell me where he has gone?

3. (a) I want to know.
   (b) He may have come.
   (a+b) I want to know whether he has come.

III. By using adverbial clause

1. (a) You must take interest in your studies.
   (b) You won't get pass marks.
   (a+b) Unless you take interest in your studies, you won't get pass marks.

2. (a) Nobody loves him.
   (b) He is a knave.
   (a+b) Nobody loves him because he is a knave.

3. (a) He flew to England.
   (b) He might search for his brother there.
   (a+b) He flew to England so that he might search for his brother there.

Exercise 3

Join each of the following pairs of sentences into one Complex Sentence containing an 'adjectival clause'.

1. (a) The bull was brought to India.
   (b) It could engage even a lion in a fight.

   ____

   ____

2. (a) This is the station.
   (b) Every train stops here for five minutes.

   ____

3. (a) This is the boat.
   (b) It has never capsized during the past five years.

   ____

   ____

4. (a) This is the boy.
   (b) His casual attitude towards studies is going to stall his success in life.

   ____

   ____

5. (a) The boy is good.
   (b) I have borrowed five hundred dollars from him.

____

6. (a) This is the road.
   (b) It leads to Nairobi.

____

7. (a) This is the girl.
   (b) Her mother is an army officer.

____

8. (a) The boa was very strong.
   (b) I saw it in the forest of America.

____

9. (a) You are not working properly.
   (b) Can you tell me the reason?

____

10. (a) The king was killed.
    (b) He was not wearing an armour.

____

Exercise 4

Join each of the following pairs of sentences into a Complex Sentence making use of a 'noun clause'.

1. (a) Do you have a gun?
   (b) I want to know it.

____

2. (a) She told me.
   (b) Her brother had been working in a factory since 1999.

____

3. (a) Why do you beg?
   (b) I want to know it.

____

4. (a) Who knocked on the door?
   (b) He asked me about it.

____

5. (a) He did not want to leave his own house at any cost.
   (b) He explained it to me.

____

____

6. (a) The earth revolves round the sun.
   (b) My teacher brought home to the students this fact.

____

____

7. (a) The jewellery box was not carried by the thief.
   (b) My uncle told me about it.

____

8. (a) John shot the winning goal.
   (b) We all know about it.

____

9. (a) Why was he not selected in school cricket eleven?
   (b) Can anybody tell me the reason?

____

____

10. (a) Maya has finished her homework.
    (b) She tells her mother about it.

____

Exercise 5

Join each of the following pairs of sentences into one Complex Sentence. Make use of an 'adverbial clause'.

1. (a) He could not climb Mount Everest.
   (b) He was afraid of high places.

____

2. (a) Wait here.
   (b) I shall come back.

____

3. (a) You cannot get success.
   (b) You have to work hard.

____

4. (a) He walked fast.
   (b) He could not reach the airport on time.

____

5. (a) The thief saw the policeman.
   (b) He ran away.

____

6. (a) He worked till late at night.
   (b) His object was to stand first in the class.

____

____

7. (a) She made an impressive speech.
   (b) She could not win the first prize.

____

____

8. (a) The python remained coiled around his neck.
   (b) It was killed later by the people.

____

____

9. (a) She typed fast.
   (b) Her object was to complete the work before sunset.

____

____

10. (a) He could not attend the meeting.
    (b) He had to fly to New Zealand.

____

UNIT 18

CONVERSION OF SENTENCES

I. Conversion of Compound Sentences into Complex Sentences

Read the following sentences carefully.

1. **Compound** : The path was slippery, yet I could manage to cross it.
   Complex : Although the path was slippery, I could manage to cross it.

2. **Compound** : Don't move or you will be shot dead.
   Complex : If you do not stop moving, you will be shot dead.

3. **Compound** : Show me your I-card or you cannot be allowed to enter the hall.
   Complex : Unless you show me your I-card, you cannot be allowed to enter the hall.

4. **Compound** : She walked fast and caught the train.
   Complex : She caught the train because she walked fast.

Exercise 1

Change the following Compound Sentences into Complex Sentences.

1. The novel was full of errors, yet the reader could manage to understand the actual story.

   ____

   ____

2. He tried hard and got success.

   ____

3. Don't tease the birds or you will be punished.

   ____

4. Give me your camera or you cannot be allowed to meet the Prime Minister.

   ____

5. He wrote a very good essay and won the first prize.

____

6. The knife was sharp and with it the child cut the mushrooms into small pieces.

____

____

7. He wept bitterly yet his mother did not buy him a kite.

____

8. The lion roared loudly yet it could not terrorize the child.

____

9. Don't disturb me or you will be thrown out of the room.

____

10. She sang sweetly and was liked by all.

____

II. Conversion of Complex Sentences into Simple Sentences

Read the following sentences carefully.

1. **Complex** : She was glad that she had won the scholarship.
   Simple : She was glad to win the scholarship.

2. **Complex** : He was so afraid that he could not give the full detail of the incident.
   Simple : He was too afraid to give the full detail of the incident.

3. **Complex** : He lost the match because he was not fully prepared.
   Simple : Being not fully prepared, he lost the match.

4. **Complex** : Although he is poor, he is kind.
   Simple : In spite of being poor, he is kind.

5. **Complex** : If you do not work hard, you cannot get success.
   Simple : You can get success only by working hard.
   Or
   You cannot get success without working hard.

Exercise 2

Change the following Complex Sentences into Simple Sentences.

1. If you do not listen to your teacher, you cannot get good marks in the examination.

2. Although he is weak in mathematics, he managed to get pass marks.

3. He was so busy that he could not attend the guests.

4. He could not attend the meeting because he got up late that morning.

5. He dived into the tank so that he might get relief from the scorching heat of the sun.

6. The girl plucked the flowers so that she might make a bouquet to present it to her teacher.

7. If he puts on a new dress, he will be selected for the new film.

8. Although it was raining heavily, he could make it to his house.

9. John was amazed how his friend had finished his dinner so fast.

10. She could not help him because she was not aware about his financial position.

III. Conversion of Compound Sentences into Simple Sentences

Read the following sentences carefully.

1. **Compound** : The thief not only beat Mr Henry but also robbed him of all his cash.
   Simple : Besides robbing Mr Henry of all his cash the thief beat him.
   Or
   Besides beating Mr Henry, the thief also robbed him of all his cash.

2. **Compound** : He finished his work and walked out of the office.
   Simple : Having finished his work he walked out of the office.

3. **Compound** : She is rich but miserly.
   Simple : In spite of her riches (or being rich) she is miserly.

4. **Compound** : The path was covered with thorns, yet we managed to cross it.
   Simple : The path, in spite of its being covered with thorns, we managed to cross it.
   Or
   We managed to cross the path in spite of its being covered with thorns.

5. **Compound** : Walk fast otherwise you may miss the flight.
   Simple : Walk fast to avoid missing the flight.

Exercise 3

Change the following Compound Sentences into Simple Sentences.

1. The train was fast, yet he got down from it quickly.

   ____

2. Don't talk otherwise you may be punished.

   ____

3. She worked hard but she could not clear the examination.

   ____

4. Not only did Robin break the chair but also he made much noise.

   ____

5. Work hard or you are going to lose your five dollars.

____

6. He ran fast but he could not win the race.

____

7. He was fat but he was very active.

____

8. You must play well or we shall lose the match.

____

9. Don't laugh or you will be thrown out of these premises.

____

10. She cooked the dish and went into the drawing-room.

____

IV. Interchange of Exclamatory and Assertive Sentences

Exclamations can be transformed into Assertions and vice versa.

A. Exclamations into Assertions

Examples

1. **Exclamatory** : What a handsome child it is!
   Assertive : The child is very handsome. **Or**, It is a very handsome child.

2. **Exclamatory** : How bad the weather was!
   Assertive : The weather was very bad.

Exercise 4

Change the following Exclamations into Assertions.

1. How ferocious this wild beast is!

____

2. What a lovely weather today is!

____

3. What a fool you are!

____

4. How big this house is!

____

5. How bad this news is!

____

6. How cold it is!

____

7. What a delicious apple this is!

____

8. How badly his head bleeds!

____

9. What a wonderful bird it is!

____

10. How beautiful this dress is!

____

B. Assertions into Exclamations

Examples

1. **Assertive** : This is a very strong dog.
   Exclamatory : How strong this dog is!

2. **Assertive** : I wish I had ten hands.
   Exclamatory : O that I had ten hands!

3. **Assertive** : You are a very good man.
   Exclamatory : What a good man you are!

4. **Assertive** : It is a matter of sorrow that I am undone.
   Exclamatory : Alas! I am undone.

Exercise 5

Change the following Assertive Sentences into Exclamatory Sentences.

1. I wish I had wings.

   ____

2. It is a matter of deep sorrow that Jack is dead.

   ____

3. This is a very beautiful animal.

   ____

4. You are a big cheat.

   ____

5. He dances very well.

   ____

6. I wish I were rich.

   ____

7. The rainbow is very beautiful.

   ____

8. The blue whale is very big.

   ____

9. She is a very intelligent girl.

   ____

10. This is a very calm place.

    ____

UNIT 19

THE INFINITIVE

A. Sometimes a clause can be replaced with an Infinitive.

Examples

1 I was surprised when I saw him coming.
I was surprised **to see him coming**.

2. They say that he is a bully.
He is said **to be a bully**.

3. She wondered how her daughter looked.
She wondered **to think how her daughter looked**.

Exercise 1

Replace the Clause with an Infinitive in each of the following sentences or insert an Infinitive where necessary.

1. They thought that he was a gentleman.

____

2. I wonder how Tina will look like in these clothes.

____

3. He worked hard that he might earn one million dollars by the end of the year.

____

4. John was the first boy who entered the hall.

____

5. It is said that he knows about future.

____

6. She sighs that she may become a play-back singer.

____

7. I'm glad that you have set up a new office in the heart of the city.

____

8. We do not expect that we shall ever lose the match.

____

9. She trembled when she saw a snake close to her.

____

10. She was delighted when she learned of her father's improved health.

____

B. With the help of Infinitives two sentences can be joined.

Examples

1. (a) He is fat.
   (b) He cannot work fast.
   He is too fat **to work** fast.
2. (a) He is intelligent.
   (b) He can solve this problem.
   He is intelligent enough **to solve** this problem.
3. (a) He is not very rich.
   (b) He cannot buy a scooter.
   He is not rich enough **to buy** a scooter.

Exercise 2

Join each of the following pairs of sentences by using Infinitives.

1. (a) She is clever.
   (b) She will overcome the obstacle.

   ____

2. (a) He is short.
   (b) He cannot touch the ceiling.

   ____

3. (a) Julie is very rich.
   (b) She can buy a new house.

   ____

4. (a) This book is very tough.
   (b) A child cannot understand it.

   ____

5. (a) He was strong.
   (b) He could give good fight to his rival.

____

6. (a) She is weak.
   (b) She cannot walk or sit properly.

____

7. (a) Sam is not very talented.
   (b) He cannot be an actor.

____

8. (a) The monkey was not very big.
   (b) It could not climb to the top of the tree.

____

9. (a) The explosion was very powerful.
   (b) It brought about a great damage to the towering buildings.

____

10. (a) This book is not very small.
    (b) No one can read it in one sitting.

____

11. (a) This room is spacious.
    (b) All these boxes can be put in it.

____

12. (a) The box was very heavy.
    (b) The boy could not carry it to the room.

____

13. (a) Mary was very busy.
    (b) She could not get time to sew your shirt.

____

14. (a) It was very cold outside.
    (b) I could not go anywhere.

____

15. (a) The weather was pleasant.
    (b) We could go for a picnic.

____

UNIT 20

PARTICIPLE CLAUSES

Read the following sentences.

1 (a) She watched the kites.
(b) They were flying.
(a+b) She watched the kites **flying**. (Present Participle is used.)

2 (a) He walked along the fence.
(b) He saw a strange stone.
(a+b) While **walking** along the fence he saw a strange stone.
(Present Participle is used.)

3. (a) He was defeated by his enemy.
(b) He decided to fly somewhere else.
(a+b) **Defeated** by his enemy, he decided to fly somewhere else.
(Past Participle is used.)

4. (a) He had finished painting the doors.
(b) He went out of the house to stroll.
(a+b) **Having finished** painting the doors, he went out of the house to stroll.
(Perfect Participle is used.)

Exercise 1

Introduce the Present Participle Clause by joining each pair of the following sentences.

1. (a) I listened to the music.
(b) It was coming from the next room.

____

2. (a) He heard a strange voice behind his head.
(b) He was going to school on the empty road.

____

3. (a) I saw the cat.
   (b) It was grooming itself.

____

4. (a) I was swimming through the ford.
   (b) I saw a starfish being carried away by the gigantic water current.

____

5. (a) I could see the flag.
   (b) It was waving in the fast blowing wind.

____

6. (a) Look at the moon.
   (b) It is shining calmly.

____

7. (a) I could hear the old man.
   (b) He was crying for help.

____

8. (a) The child rolled down the stairs.
   (b) He was ascending the stairs with bounding steps.

____

9. (a) The warriors took out their guns.
   (b) They started running towards the border.

____

10. (a) She was looking towards the door.
    (b) She saw her father entering.

____

11. (a) She smelt the cake.
    (b) It was burning.

____

12. (a) The old man sat under the tree.
    (b) He was mumbling away to himself.

____

13. (a) The maid swept the floor.
    (b) She found a five-cent coin.

____

14. (a) They watched the train.
    (b) It was running at a terrible speed.

____

15. (a) I can see the boy.
    (b) He is dancing merrily.

____

Exercise 2

Introduce the Past Participle Clause by joining each pair of the following sentences.

1. (a) He was deceived by his friends.
   (b) He decided to leave the town.

____

____

2. (a) He was rejected by all.
   (b) He decided not to talk to anybody in future.

____

____

3. (a) The dog was terrified by the zooming sound of the landing aeroplane.
   (b) It began to run about.

____

____

4. (a) The prince was condemned by all.
   (b) He decided to apologise to the people.

____

____

5. (a) The guerrillas were beaten back by the army.
   (b) They decided to skulk in the hideouts in the alpine ravines.

____

____

6. (a) He was amazed at the beauty of the wild animal.
   (b) He decided to have a snap of it.

____

____

7. (a) In the dark the boy got hit against the wall.
   (b) He went unconscious.

____

____

8. (a) The motel is situated on the highway.
   (b) It is a big resting place for motorists.

____

____

9. (a) The stone was thrown with great force.
   (b) It struck the thief on the head.

____

____

10. (a) The dry leaves were driven aside the road by the strong wind.
    (b) They began to heap up.

____

____

Exercise 3

Introduce the Perfect Clause joining each of the pairs of the following sentences.

1. (a) She had made dough.
   (b) She was ready to bake a big cake.

____

____

2. (a) The boy broke the glass.
   (b) He went out of the house to play.

____

3. (a) The girl applied a dash of lipstick on her lips.
   (b) She looked at her reflection in the mirror.

____

____

4. (a) The officer attended the meeting.
   (b) He went to Tokyo later.

____

____

5. (a) The burglar broke into the house.
   (b) He looted whatever he was able to carry (with himself).

____

____

6. (a) The driver applied the brakes suddenly.
   (b) He got down the lorry.

____

____

7. (a) The lizard feasted on a swarm of mosquitoes.
   (b) It went back into the hole.

____

____

8. (a) She had washed the clothes.
   (b) She went into the kitchen.

____

____

9. (a) The child had cut the paper into small pieces.
   (b) He put the scissors back on the shelf.

____

____

10. (a) The boys plucked the flowers.
    (b) They scurried out of the garden.

____

____

UNIT 21

WORD FORMATION

Look at the following words.

(a)	**dis**arranged	**un**covered
(b)	friend**ship**	king**dom**

The bold element given in each of the words under (a) is called a **Prefix** because it is placed before the remaining part of the word. Similarly the bold element given in each of the words under (b) is called a **Suffix** because it is placed at the end of the remaining part of the word.

Prefixes

Uses of Prefixes in different words:

Prefixes	Meanings	Words
a-	on, in	ajar, asleep, aboard
ambi-	on both sides	ambidextrous
ante-	before, preceding	antedate
anti-	opposite, against	antiaircraft
contra-	against	contradict
de-	down	dethrone
dis-	-remove -to denote absence of an action or state	disbud disaffirm
ex-	out of	extract
extra-	beyond, outside of	extraordinary
fore-	before	forecast
hemi-	half	hemisphere
hyper-	above normal	hypertension
hypo-	below normal	hypotension
mis-	wrong, wrongly	mislead
over-	above	overflow
pre-	before	predict

re-	back, again	regain, restore
un-	not	untrue
un-	to reverse an action	unfold
under-	below, beneath	underground, underpressure

Suffixes

Uses of Suffixes in different words:

Suffixes	**Meanings**	**Words**
-ana	denoting plural nouns associated with a person, place, etc.	Americana
-asis	making names of the diseases	psoriasis
-ation	forming nouns showing action	hesitation
-ative	forming adjectives each denoting a character	talkative
-dom	-forming nouns each denoting a state or condition -denoting status -denoting domain	freedom earldom, kingdom
-ed	having	learned
-en	made of	golden
-ful	full of	joyful
-ish	-somewhat -nationality of	yellowish Irish, Swedish
-ly	like	widely
-less	without	faultless, flavourless
-ness	formation of abstract nouns	nervousness
-ock	forming nouns with diminutive sense	bullock
-ward	inclining to	forward

FORMATION OF NOUNS

Nouns can be formed from different parts of speech.

1. *Formation of Nouns From Adjectives*

Adjectives	Nouns
able	ability
absent	absence
accurate	accuracy
active	activity
actual	actuality
adequate	adequacy
barren	barrenness
bitter	bitterness
black	black/blackness
blunt	bluntness
bold	boldness
bright	brightness
broad	breadth
busy	business
calm	calmness
careful	carefulness
casual	casualty
cautious	cautiousness
cheap	cheapness
certain	certainty
civil	civility
close	closeness
coward	cowardice
cruel	cruelty
dark	darkness
deaf	deafness
deep	depth
dear	dearth
devious	deviousness
dense	density
equal	equality
exact	exactness
false	falseness

Adjectives	Nouns
fast	fastness
feeble	feebleness
fine	fineness
foolish	foolishness
forceful	forcefulness
frank	frankness
free	freedom
fresh	freshness
gay	gaiety
generous	generosity
giddy	giddiness
glossy	gloss
good	goodness
grand	grandeur
great	greatness
happy	happiness
hard	hardship
harmless	harmlessness
haughty	haughtiness
health	healthiness
hearty	heartiness
heavy	heaviness
holy	holiness
honest	honesty
ideal	idealism
idle	idleness
ignorant	ignorance
ill	illness
impersonal	impersonality
infant	infancy
inferior	inferiority
innocent	innocence
lame	lameness
large	largeness

Adjectives	Nouns
lawless	lawlessness
lazy	laziness
lively	liveliness
local	locality
long	length
loyal	loyalty
mean	meanness
merciless	mercilessness
mild	mildness
moral	morality
necessary	necessity
nervous	nervousness
new	newness
noble	nobility
nude	nudity
obedient	obedience
obvious	obviousness
patient	patience
poor	poverty
popular	popularity
private	privacy
pure	purity
reliable	reliability
regular	regularity
rich	richness
rival	rivalry
round	roundness
royal	royalty
safe	safety
secret	secrecy
short	shortness
soft	softness
special	speciality
stupid	stupidity
sure	surety
sweet	sweetness
warm	warmness
weak	weakness
wise	wisdom

2. *Formation of Nouns From Verb*

Verbs	Nouns
able	ability
abhor	abhorrence
acquire	acquisition
act	action
add	addition
adore	adoration
advise	advice
appear	appearance
apply	application
approve	approval
arrive	arrival
bear	bier
bind	bond
bless	bliss
bore	boredom
broaden	breadth
build	building
carry	carriage
choose	choice
close	closure
collect	collection
collide	collision
complete	completion
conform	conformity
convert	conversion
deliver	delivery
descend	descent
develop	development
dictate	dictation
digest	digestion
direct	direction
distract	distraction
educate	education
elope	elopement
employ	employment
enforce	enforcement

Verbs	Nouns
enjoy	enjoyment
envelop	envelope
exist	existence
gamble	gambling
give	gift
go	gait
govern	governance
grade	gradation
graduate	graduation
guide	guidance
hate	hatred
heal	health
hesitate	hesitation
hold	holding
laugh	laughter
leak	leakage
learn	learning
lend	loan
link	linkage
live	living
lose	loss
make	making
measure	measurement
meet	meeting
mix	mixture
mock	mockery
modernize	modernization
move	movement
navigate	navigation
nominate	nomination
notify	notification
nourish	nourishment
obey	obedience
object	objection
observe	observation

Verbs	Nouns
obsess	obsession
obstruct	obstruction
occur	occurrence
open	opener
oppress	oppression
opt	option
participate	participation
pay	payment
plant	plantation
predicate	predication
predict	prediction
prefer	preference
project	projection
punish	punishment
realize	realization
refer	reference
refuse	refusal
relieve	relief
restrict	restriction
restore	restoration
resume	resumption
run	race
say	saying
see	sight
serve	service
solve	solution
speak	speech
steal	stealth
stop	stoppage
suffer	suffering
suspect	suspicion
tax	taxation
tell	talk
tend	tendency
trace	track
train	training
translate	translation

3. ***Formation of Adjectives From Nouns***

Nouns	Adjectives
access	accessible
acid	acidic
advantage	advantageous
adventure	adventurous
air	airy
anger	angry
anxiety	anxious
apprehension	apprehensive
art	artful
awe	awful
bag	baggy
balm	balmy
beauty	beautiful
blood	bloody
body	bodily
book	bookish
boy	boyish
burden	burdensome
care	careful
caution	cautious
child	childish
circle	circular
class	classic
clerk	clerical
climate	climatic
comfort	comfortable
cone	conical
contempt	contemptible
courtesy	courteous
coward	cowardly
danger	dangerous
day	daily
dazzle	dazzling
death	deadly
decency	decent
decoration	decorative
destruction	destructive

Nouns	Adjectives
dew	dewy
duty	dutiful
earth	earthly
ease	easy
east	eastern
economy	economical
element	elementary
emotion	emotional
enigma	enigmatic
envy	envious
excess	excessive
faith	faithful
fancy	fanciful
fate	fateful
father	fatherly
fault	faulty
favour	favourable
fear	fearsome
fiction	fictional
film	filmy
fog	foggy
fun	funny
fury	furious
gas	gaseous
ghost	ghostly
glass	glassy
glory	glorious
god	god-like
gold	golden
grass	grassy
greed	greedy
grief	grievous
gum	gummy
hair	hairy
harm	harmful
heat	hot
heaven	heavenly
hero	heroic
hill	hilly

Nouns	Adjectives
history	historical
home	homely
hope	hopeful
horn	horny
ice	icy
idiom	idiomatic
ignorance	ignorant
image	imaginary
influence	influential
jerk	jerky
joke	jocular
joy	joyful
jump	jumpy
justice	just
king	kingly
knight	knightly
knot	knotty
labour	laborious
law	lawful
leisure	leisurely
life	lifeless
line	linear, lineal
lord	lordly
love	lovable, lovely
mass	massive
memory	memorable
metal	metallic
method	methodical
might	mighty
milk	milky
mirth	mirthful
mischief	mischievous
miser	miserable
moment	momentary
mother	motherly, maternal
nation	national

Nouns	Adjectives
nature	natural
navy	naval
need	needful
neglect	neglectful
nerve	nervous
night	nightly
notice	noticeable
novel	novelette
number	numeral
obsession	obsessional
occasion	occasional
occupation	occupational
ocean	oceanic
offence	offensive
officer	official
oil	oily
origin	original
palace	palatial
peace	peaceful
people	populous, popular
person	personal
pity	pitiful
play	playful
poet	poetic
pole	polar
power	powerful
pride	proud
progress	progressive
read	readable
reason	reasonable
rectangle	rectangular
reliance	reliable
rest	restful
right	righteous
rose	rosy
rust	rusty
sale	saleable
sand	sandy

Nouns	Adjectives
scene	scenic
scholar	scholarly
science	scientific
scorn	scornful
skill	skillful
space	spacious
sport	sportive
star	starry
storm	stormy
talk	talkative
term	terminal
text	textual
theatre	theatrical
thirst	thirsty
time	timely
trouble	troublesome
value	valuable
verb	verbal
vice	vicious
victory	victorious
village	rural
voice	vocal
war	warlike
watch	watchful
water	watery
wind	windy
world	worldly
year	yearly
youth	youthful

4. *Formation of Verbs*

Words	Verbs
able	enable
abundant	abound
access	accede
base	debase
bath	bathe
beauty	beautify
bed	embed
bitter	embitter
breath	breathe
broad	broaden
camp	encamp
centre	centralize
certain	certify
circle	encircle
civil	civilize
clean	cleanse
cloth	clothe
colony	colonize
danger	endanger
dear	endear
different	differ
drop	drip
false	falsify
fat	fatten
feeble	enfeeble
firm	confirm
flat	flatten
fond	fondle
full	fill
glad	gladden
glass	glaze
glory	glorify
grass	graze
hand	handle
haste	hasten
hateful	hate
head	behead
high	heighten
humble	humiliate
large	enlarge
life	live

Words	Verbs
long	longthen
mad	madden
mean	demean
memory	memorize
moist	moisten
nest	nestle
new	renew
people	populate
poor	impoverish
port	import, export
prison	imprison
public	publish
real	realize
red	redden
rich	enrich

Words	Verbs
safe	save
service	serve
sharp	sharpen
short	shorten
sick	sicken
special	specialize
speech	speak
sure	ensure
tale	tell
thick	thicken
vacancy	vacate
vapour	evaporate
various	vary
veritable	verify
weak	weaken
web	weave
wide	widen

UNIT 22

SYNONYMS AND ANTONYMS

SYNONYMS

The words which have almost the same meaning are called Synonyms

admit	allow, confess
adoring	loving
adversary	opponent
affect	influence
afraid	frightened
aged	old
aim	target
amity	friendship
announce	declare
anxious	worried
arrogant	stubborn
artificial	false
assurance	promise
astounding	surprising
baffle	confuse
barbarous	cruel
bark	shout
bawl	shout
bear	tolerate
beautiful	attractive
benevolent	generous
bicker	squabble
bid	attempt
booty	loot
cajole	coax
calm	peaceful
capable	skilled
carefree	worriless
careful	worried
cast	shed
catastrophe	disaster
catch	capture
catching	infectious
certain	sure
choke	strangle
competent	skilled
damage	destroy
damp	wet
dash	sprint
decay	rot
deceive	mislead
decline	fall
definite	sure/certain
depression	hollow
devastating	destructive
dexterous	skilful
difficult	tough
eclipse	outshine
effectual	effective
efficacy	effectiveness
elevate	raise
embrace	hug
enchant	charm, bewitch
endure	last
enlarge	elaborate
enormous	great
entire	whole
entreat	beg
evaluate	assess
fabricate	manufacture
fade	dull
fair	acceptable

faithful	loyal
fake	false
fantastic	brilliant
fascinating	charming
fizzle	hiss
flare	erupt
flatly	absolutely
flourish	thrive
foil	thwart
fondle	caress
gain	obtain
garish	showy
garrulous	talkative
gather	collect
generous	kind
genteel	polite
giant	gigantic
glamorous	charming
gleam	shine
glittering	shining
gloomy	dark
glorious	beautiful
handy	useful
happy	contented
hate	avert
haunting	evocative
hazard	endanger
hazy	vague
hesitation	doubt
hilarious	amusing
holocaust	massacre
horror	fear
hostile	unfriendly
huffy	annoyed
hurl	flung
idle	lazy
idyllic	happy
ignorant	uneducated
illegal	lawless
illude	mislead
illuminate	lighten
illusive	deceptive

imitate	copy
immature	developing
immediate	instant
immortal	perpetual
impeccable	perfect
impel	drive
impish	mischievous
jaunt	excursion
jocund	cheerful
jolly	happy
jumble	confuse, mixup
juvenile	childish
keen	eager
kind	generous
knotty	intricate
knowledge	intelligence
lackadaisical	indolent
laconic	brief
lament	mourn
lampoon	criticize
lanky	tall
lasting	enduring
laudable	appreciable
laughable	ridiculous
lavish	extravagant
lethal	deadly
lewd	obscene
libel	defame
limpid	vivid, clear
lissome	supple
macabre	terrifying
magnanimous	generous
magnificent	attractive
majesty	grandeur
major	important
malevolent	malicious
manipulate	handle
marvellous	wonderful
massive	plentiful, large
meek	gentle
melodious	sweet

menace	threat
nadir	bottom
naive	artless
nasty	unpleasant
nebulous	cloudy, hazy
nefarious	atrocious
negate	nullify
negotiable	discussable
nervous	puzzled
nutritious	nourishing
obedience	submission
objectionable	unpleasant, offensive
obnoxious	unpleasant
obscure	vague
obstruct	hinder
obvious	clear
offensive	repulsive
operate	manage
oppose	resist
optimistic	hopeful
opulent	wealthy
outstanding	prominent, excellent
pale	feeble
pare	trim
pathetic	sad
peaceful	calm
pensive	melancholy
penurious	poor
perfidious	deceitful
perplex	confuse
petty	trivial
placid	calm
profound	great
prudent	wise
rapacious	greedy
reasonable	sensible
rebuke	scold
refuse	rubbish
reject	dismiss
remarkable	attractive
repress	prevent
repulsive	disgustful
restore	return
robust	strong
rudimentary	basic
sabotage	destroy
sagacious	wise
savage	cruel
scanty	insufficient
scratchy	rough
sensible	wise
shrink	contract
significant	important
silly	foolish
sonorous	ringing
splendid	impressive
stout	strong
tangible	perceptible
tart	acidic
tedious	dull
terrific	grand
thrill	excite
titanic	big
tremendous	great
ulterior	concealed
umpteen	countless
uncivil	disrespectful
unending	endless
uproar	clamour
urgent	compelling
utmost	chief
vague	obscure
vain	arrogant
valid	acceptable
vast	boundless
verbose	prolix
vicious	bad
vigorous	active

vivacious	cheerful
vivid	clear
warm	heated

ANTONYMS

The words with opposite meanings

abate	boost, increase
abhor	love
able	unable
absurd	logical
acute	dull
adore	hate
alert	unaware
anxious	calm
ardent	cold
attract	disgust
avid	lukewarm
baffle	explain
ban	allow
bare	concealed
bashful	arrogant
beautiful	ugly
becoming	awful
benign	harsh
bold	cowardly
brash	cautious
breezy	calm
brief	detailed
bright	dull
calamitous	beneficial
calling	curse
calm	disturbed
canny	uncanny
capable	incapable
care	pleasure
catch	drop
caution	rashness
cheerful	depress/ gloomy
chief	minor
chubby	thin
clear	cloudy
clumsy	adopt
colossal	minute
dangerous	harmless
decent	frankness
decline	accept
deep	shallow
definite	fuzzy
delicious	unpleasant
delight	disgust
deny	accept
determination	hesitation
detest	adore
devotion	inattention
difficult	easy
diligent	lazy
earger	indifferent
effective	inactive
efficient	inefficient
elegant	clumsy
eligible	ineligible
eloquent	hesitant
eminent	infamous
emphatic	tame
encourage	discourage
energetic	lazy
enough	lacking
enthusiastic	cool
evident	doubtful
expensive	cheap
facility	awkwardness
fair	unfair
faithful	disloyal
fake	true
false	true
famous	notorious
fascinate	bore
feeble	strong
fine	poor
frank	cunning/shy
fraud	honesty
gallant	fearful
garnish	spoil
generous	greedy
gentle	aggressive
get	loose

gigantic	tiny
give	take
glad	displeased
glorious	gloomy
good	bad
great	small
hamper	encourage
handy	clumsy
happy	sad
hard	soft
harsh	gentle
haste	care
hate	love
haughty	humble
hectic	calm
homogeneous	heterogeneous
horrible	attractive
huffy	calm
idle	industrious
ignorant	brilliant
immoral	honourable
impel	dissuade
imposing	mean
imprudent	cautions
impudent	polite
incisive	dull
incorrigible	corrigible
incredulous	credulous
indolent	active
jolly	morose
judicious	imprudent
jumpy	calm
just	unjust
keen	lukewarm
key	minor
kindly	cruelly
lack	abundance
lackadaisical	diligent
laconic	detailed
lavish	miserly
lazy	diligent
legible	illegible
liberal	limited
lifeless	alive
like	dislike
lucid	unclear
magnificent	modest
main	minor
majestic	modest/mean
major	minor
malicious	friendly
meek	bold
memorable	forgettable
meritorious	dishonourable
merry	clean
mighty	feeble
mild	stormy
morose	happy
musty	fresh
nadir	apex
nasty	clean
nave	artful
nefarious	honest
nervous	bold
noble	dishonest
notable	concealed
obedient	disobedient
object	accept
obscure	clear
obvious	dark
odious	charming
onerous	easy
openly	privately
original	copied
outlandish	familiar
overt	covert
passionate	passionless
peaceful	hostile
peculiar	ordinary
peerless	inferior
piquant	dull
pithy	garrulous

plausible	impossible
plump	lean
pompous	impotent
precise	careless
pressing	routine
radical	minor
rapid	slow
rare	frequent
rash	canny
readable	illegible
real	fake
rebuke	approve
reject	accept
remarkable	ordinary
resist	yield
rewarding	boring
sallow	rosy
sanguine	gloomy
scandalous	decent
secret	candid
sensible	ignorant
serene	anxious
sever	mild
shaky	steady
sharp	dull
shrewd	dull
significant	insignificant
silly	acute
tactful	tactless
talkative	quiet
tarry	hurry
tasty	insipid
tempting	unattractive
tenacious	flexible
tepid	eager
timid	aggressive
touchy	cheerful
tribute	complaint
unabashed	abashed
unbecoming	decent
uncanny	canny
unethical	honest
valiant	fearful
vast	limited
verbose	brief
viscous	docile
vivacious	boring/dull
vulgar	elegant

UNIT 23

PHRASAL VERBS

It is very usual to place prepositions or adverbs after a verb to get a particular meaning.

Account

- **account for** : give a good reason for
  You have to account for every penny you spend towards this project.
- **on account of** : because of
  Yesterday he could not attend the meeting on account of ill health.
- **give a good account of oneself** : perform well
  Our team gave a good account of it in the last match.

Answer

- **answer back** : to speak rudely to somebody particularly when he/she is criticizing you

  You should not have answered your brother back. What he was saying to you was for your benefit.
- **answer for somebody** : to say that somebody else will do something or not
  I agree, but I can't answer for my brother.
- **answer for something** : to promise that somebody has a particular quality
  I can answer for his sincerity.
- **answer to somebody** : to give required explanation to somebody
  All the bank clerks answer to the manager.

Bare

- **with one's bare hands** : without using a weapon
  The hunter killed the wolf with his bare hands.
- **bare one's soul** : to tell somebody your deepest and most private feelings
  Don't hesitate and bare your soul to me.

Beat

- **beat about the bush** : to talk about something meaninglessly for a long time
  Boys, don't keep beating about the bush. Go home and concentrate on your books.
- **beat a retreat** : to go away back on perceiving danger, etc.
  The enemy beat a retreat when it found our forces alert at the border.
- **beat down** : shine brightly
  At noon the sun beats down at open places.
- **beat off** : force somebody back
  The enemy was beaten off.

Break

- **break down** : to stop working because of some fault
  The electric supply has broken down.
- **break something down** : to make something fall
  The police broke down the door and captured the criminal.
- **break off** : to stop speaking for a few moments
  She broke off in the middle of her speech.
- **break up** : to separate into smaller pieces or parts
  The waves broke up on the rocks.
- **break out** : spread fast
  Cholera has broken out in the village. **Or**,
  War broke out on 19th Dec. last year.

Bring

- **bring somebody round** : to persuade somebody to agree to your opinion
  I have to try hard to bring him round.
- **bring something forward** : to produce some documents etc. for discussion
  The minister brought the matter forward.
- **bring up** : to educate and train a child
  She was brought up by her uncle.
- **bring something up** : to raise
  I shall bring this matter up in the next meeting.

Call

- **call in** : to call
  The doctor was called in.
- **call at** : to stop at a place for a short time
  Yesterday, I called at the hospital and met my uncle.

- **call on** : to meet a person
  He called on all his friends in the area.
- **call for** : demand
  They called up immediate installation of computer in the office.
- **call of** : abandon something
  The workers called off the strike.
- **call out** : to summon
  When the police failed to control the mob, the troops had to be called out.

Carry

- **carry on** : to continue
  You should carry on with your books.
- **carry out** : to obey
  Miss Mary has to carry out the manager's orders.
- **carry something through** : to complete successfully
  Although the task was tough, Tony managed to carry it through.

Come

- **come across** : find by chance
  When I was looking for my gold ring I came across an old coin.
- **come in** : to enter
  Please come in.
- **come out** : be revealed
  All truth about the matter came out at last.
- **come round** : recover from illness, etc.
  She was badly wounded and was unconscious, but soon she came round.
- **come along** : to arrive
  When the right opportunity comes along, we should not miss it.

Cut

- **cut down** : reduce
  Our company has decided to cut down the prices of its products.
- **cut somebody down** : to kill somebody
  He was cut down by a rival, arrow.
- **cut off** : disconnect
  The electricity board cut off their electric supply to the village.

  be cut out for something : to have the abilities needed for something
  You are not cut out for the career of a doctor.

Draw

- **draw back** : recoil
  It is too late to draw back now, as everything is ready.
- **draw something from somebody** : to take from a particular source
  Tony drew inspiration from the life history of his most lovable leader.

Drive

- **drive (somebody or something) away** : to take somebody or something away in a vehicle
  Sophia drove the car away through the dense forest. **Or,**
  The kidnappers drove the businessman away to an unknown place.
- **drive off** : to leave
  The thief drove off in a car.
- **drive on** : to continue driving
  Don't stop, drive on!

Fall

- **fall away** : to become gradually smaller or to disappear
  All the greenery in the village has fallen away since we visited it last-time.
- **fall back** : to turn back
  The enemy fell back as our troops moved forward.
- **fall behind** : to fail to keep level with somebody
  The child fell behind the group he was walking with.
- **fall through** : fail to materialize
  His scheme fell through for want of funds.

Get

- **get about** : circulate
  The news got about that Mr Simon had won a jackpot.
- **get at somebody** : to keep criticizing
  Mrs Maria is always getting at you.
- **get away** : to have a holiday
  We are hoping to get away for a month in Switzerland.
- **get back** : return
  I shall get back home at about 9 p.m.
- **get into something** : to board
  Henry managed to get into the jam packed train.
- **get up** : wake rise
  Parker daily gets up at 7 o'clock.

- **get on** : used to ask about how well somebody is doing with a particular subject
  Diana is getting on very well with her studies.

Go

- **go about something** : to continue
  In spite of war, the people in the cities went about their business as usual.
- **go after somebody** : to follow
  The police went after a gang of burglars.
- **go against somebody** : not to be in favour of somebody
  The decision went against Mr David.
- **go at somebody** : attack
  He went at the boy ruthlessly.
- **go away** : to leave a place
  The dog went away to its kennel.
- **go on** : to continue
  Go on till you find a turn.
- **go back** : return
  The students started going back to the hostel on the announcement of a holiday.
- **go back on** : to fail to keep a promise
  Rosy never goes back on her word.

Give

- **give away** : to distribute
  The chief guest gave away the prizes.
- **give in** : to yield
  The bridge gave in under the heavy weight of vehicles.
- **give out** : to release
  The automobile gave out poisonous fumes.
- **give up** : to abandon
  He has given up smoking.

Hold

- **hold on** : wait
  Please hold on for a minute. Mr Hood will be soon along.
- **hold out something** : to offer a hope
  The doctor held out little hope for John's recovery.
- **hold up** : to remain strong
  He is holding up well in spite of so many problems.

Keep

- **keep on** : continue
  Lily kept on talking though she was ordered to keep mum.
- **keep off** : refrain from
  Keep off the marshy tract, as it is infested with snakes.
- **keep somebody back** : hinder
  Frequent raining kept him back.
- **keep out** : stay outside
  Keep out, please.
- **keep something back** : to refuse to tell something
  You should not keep anything back from us.

Lay

- **lay something aside** : to put something to one side
  He laid aside his pillow and launched out of the bed.
- **lay something down** : to put something down
  He laid down the pillow on the bed.
- **lay about somebody** : to attack
  A gang of bullies laid about him with iron rods.

Look

- **look after** : to take care
  You should look after your old parents.
- **look at something** : to examine something closely
  Your face is growing pale. I think some specialist ought to look at it.
- **look for something** : to hope
  I am looking for some improvement in his behaviour..
- **look into something** : to examine something
  The new police inspector will look into the matter.
- **look out** : to watch something when there is some danger ahead
  Look out! There is a snake on the way.
- **look out for something** : to search
  I'll look out for the old coins for you.

Make

- **make up** : to complete the deficiency
  She will make up her deficiency in studies.
- **make something out** : to complete a document
  She made out a demand draft for $ 5000.

- **make towards something** : to start walking
  He made towards the door.
- **make out** : to manage to see something
  She could hear the voice but she could not make out the matter being discussed.

Move

- **move off** : to start
  The green signal being given, the train moved off.
- **move on to something** : to start doing something
  Let us move on to the next item on the agenda.
- **to move away from something** : to change the topic, etc.
  We should not move away from the famine problem until we are able to find out a solution to it.

Open

- **open out** : become bigger
  This street opens out into a square at the end.
- **open up** : to start
  I open up my shop at about 9 a.m.

Pull

- **pull away** : to move away from something or some place
  As the car pulled away, I at once crossed the road.
- **pull something down** : to demolish
  The authorities have ordered to pull down all the illegal buildings in the area.
- **pull up** : to stop
  Lily pulled up the car at the square.
- **pull through** : to become better
  The doctor hopes that Miss Mary will pull through illness.
- **pull ahead of something/somebody** : to move in front of
  All the motorbikes were running at the same level but as there came a bend on their way, one of the motorbikes pulled ahead.

Put

- **put something at** : to calculate something
  The total loss to the firm is put at 5 million dollars.
- **put something back** : to return
  Read the book and put it back on the table.

- **put something by** : to lay by or save money for future
  Mr John put by about ten thousand dollars for his daughter's education.
- **put off** : to postpone
  The meeting was put off till the next day.
- **put on** : to wear
  Put on your shirt or you can have a cold.
- **put something through** : to continue with something and complete a plan
  They managed to put the work on a particular bacterium through and got startling results.

Take

- **take off :** to remove
  Dolly took off her shoes before entering the room.
- **take something in** : to absorb by swallowing away or breathing
  Mrs Maya took in a deep breath.
- **take something out** : to remove
  The dentist managed to take out his decayed tooth.
- **take up something** : to use an amount of time or space
  It will take a lot of time to complete this job.

UNIT 24

SOME COMMON ERRORS

Given below are some of the errors commonly made by the students.

1. (a) The road is closed for **renovation**. (Incorrect)
   (b) The road is closed for **repair**. (Correct)

2. (a) The theatre is closed for **repair**. (Incorrect)
   (b) The theatre is closed for **repairs/renovation**. (Correct)

3. (a) My **older** brother is a doctor. (Incorrect)
   (b) My **elder** brother is a doctor. (Correct)

4. (a) You should pay the entire amount **by** cash. (Incorrect)
   (b) You should pay the entire amount **in** cash. (Correct)

5. (a) Please pay **in** cheque. (Incorrect)
   (b) Please pay **by** cheque. (Correct)

6. (a) Do you remember the **alphabets** of English? (Incorrect)
   (b) Do you remember the **alphabet** of English? (Correct)

7. (a) Pakistani forces attacked **on the** Indian army. (Incorrect)
   (b) Pakistani forces attacked **the** Indian army. (Correct)

8. (a) Which pen is the **best** of the two? (Incorrect)
   (b) Which pen is the **better** of the two? (Correct)

9. (a) There is a portrait of Mahatma Gandhi **at** page eight. (Incorrect)
   (b) There is a portrait of Mahatma Gandhi **on** page eight. (Correct)

10. (a) Please open your books **on** page five. (Incorrect)
    (b) Please open your books **at** page five. (Correct)

11. (a) The news **are** not true. (Incorrect)
    (b) The news **is** not true. (Correct)

12. (a) The boy is five **year** old. (Incorrect)
    (b) The boy is five **years** old. (Correct)

13. (a) Tony is a five **years** old boy. (Incorrect)
    (b) Tony is a five **year** old boy. (Correct)

14. (a) Mr Robert entered **into the hall**. (Incorrect)
    (b) Mr Robert entered **the hall**. (Correct)

15. (a) We enjoyed **at the party**. (Incorrect)
    (b) We enjoyed **ourselves at the party**. (Correct)

16. (a) There is no **place** on the bench. (Incorrect)
    (b) There is no **room** on the bench. (Correct)

17. (a) He was **too** glad to see his son. (Incorrect)
    (b) He was **very** glad to see his son. (Correct)

18. (a) **The milk** is essential for health. (Incorrect)
    (b) **Milk** is essential for health. (Correct)

19. (a) Jack does not **listen** anybody. (Incorrect)
    (b) Jack does not **listen to** anybody. (Correct)

20. (a) His pants **is** loose. (Incorrect)
    (b) His pants **are** loose. (Correct)

21. (a) The furniture in the room **are** of a good quality. (Incorrect)
    (b) The furniture in the room **is** of a good quality. (Correct)

22. (a) Please **wait** me. (Incorrect)
    (b) Please **wait for** me. (Correct)

23. (a) Please **wait for** a minute. (Incorrect)
    (b) Please **wait** a minute. (Correct)

24. (a) If you **will sing** a song, I shall give you a fifty-dollar note. (Incorrect)
    (b) If you **sing** a song, I shall give you a fifty-dollar note. (Correct)

25. (a) When he **will come**, I shall convey this message to him. (Incorrect)
    (b) When he **comes**, I shall convey this message to him. (Correct)

26. (a) The boy **which** met us in the hall is my fast friend. (Incorrect)
    (b) The boy **who** met us in the hall is my fast friend. (Correct)

27. (a) The Prime Minister along with his Cabinet **are** walking out of the hall. (Incorrect)
    (b) The Prime Minister along with his cabinet **is** walking out of the hall. (Correct)

28. (a) How hot **is it**! (Incorrect)
    (b) How hot **it is**! (Correct)

29. (a) I don't know why **is he** crying. (Incorrect)
    (b) I don't know **why he is** crying. (Correct)

30. (a) I **have met** him yesterday. (Incorrect)
    (b) I **met** him yesterday. (Correct)

31. (a) He **has bought** this bike five years ago. (Incorrect)
    (b) He **bought** this bike five years ago. (Correct)

32. (a) The gardener **is** watering the plants since morning. (Incorrect)
    (b) The gardener **has been** watering the plants since morning. (Correct)

33. (a) The police **searched for** the room. **They were looking for some important documents**. (Incorrect)
    (b) The police **searched** the room **for some important documents**. (Correct)

34. (a) Mr Gomes died **from** cancer. (Incorrect)
    (b) Mr Gomes died **of** cancer. (Correct)

35. (a) Our class **is consisting** of thirty students. (Incorrect)
    (b) Our class **consists** of thirty students. (Correct)

36. (a) The USA **is comprising of** many states. (Incorrect)
    (b) The USA **comprises** many states. (Correct)

37. (a) Somebody **knocked** the door. (Incorrect)
    (b) Somebody **knocked at/on** the door. (Correct)

38. (a) He made us **to laugh**. (Incorrect)
    (b) He made us **laugh**. (Correct)

39. (a) He dare not **to touch** my bag. (Incorrect)
    (b) He dare not **touch** my bag. (Correct)

40. (a) You need not **to come** with us. (Incorrect)
    (b) You need not **come** with us. (Correct)

41. (a) He is weak **at** English. (Incorrect)
(b) He is weak **in** English. (Correct)

42. (a) She is good **in** Mathematics. (Incorrect)
(b) She is good **at** Mathematics. (Correct)

43. (a) Mrs Rosy **signed on** the paper. (Incorrect)
(b) Mrs Rosy **signed** the paper. (Correct)
Or
Mrs Rosy **put her signature on** the paper. (Correct)

44. (a) The **sceneries** of Kashmir is charming. (Incorrect)
(b) The **scenery** of Kashmir is charming. (Correct)

45. (a) Lily is often **playing** the piano but today she is playing the violin. (Incorrect)
(b) Lily often **plays** the piano but today she is playing the violin. (Correct)

46. (a) I am going to London to see one of my **friend**. (Incorrect)
(b) I am going to London to see one of my **friends**. (Correct)

47. (a) What **are** the latest news? (Incorrect)
(b) What **is** the latest news? (Correct)

48. (a) Neither Jack nor his brothers **has** found any gold rings here. (Incorrect)
(b) Neither Jack nor his brothers **have** found any gold rings here. (Correct)

49. (a) Neither his friends nor he **have** received any letters this morning. (Incorrect)
(b) Neither his friends nor he **has** received any letters this morning. (Correct)

50. (a) Either John or his relatives **has** rights to demolish this building. (Incorrect)
(b) Either John or his relatives **have** rights to demolish this building. (Correct)

51. (a) Either his parents or he **have** received a cheque from the bank. (Incorrect)
(b) Either his parents or he **has** received a cheque from the bank. (Correct)

52. (a) Neither of the boys **were** allowed to attend the class. (Incorrect)
(b) Neither of the boys **was** allowed to attend the class. (Correct)

53. (a) This pup has no kennel to **live**. (Incorrect)
(b) This pup has no kennel to **live in**. (Correct)

54. (a) Both of the boys **was** punished by the teacher. (Incorrect)
(b) Both of the boys **were** punished by the teacher. (Correct)

55. (a) She insisted **me to sit down on the chair**. (Incorrect)
    (b) She insisted **on my sitting on the chair**. (Correct)

56. (a) Having **do** his homework, he walked out of the house to play. (Incorrect)
    (b) Having **done** his homework, he walked out of the house to play. (Correct)

57. (a) Please give me **a bread**. (Incorrect)
    (b) Please give me **a slice/piece of bread**. (Correct)

58. (a) We learn our lesson word **by** word. (Incorrect)
    (b) We learn our lesson word **for** word. (Correct)

59. (a) I as well as you **are** to blame. (Incorrect)
    (b) I as well as you **am** to blame. (Correct)

60. (a) I **can** jump over this wall when I was young. (Incorrect)
    (b) I **could** jump over this wall when I was young. (Correct)

UNIT 25

MISCELLANEOUS COMMUNICATIVE SKILLS

Telephonic Messages

Read the following telephonic conversation between Alex and Sam. Alex is about to leave and will not be able to meet Henry (his brother). He leaves a message for Henry. Prepare his message in not more than 50 words.

Alex	:	Hello! Who's there?
Sam	:	This is Sam speaking, Henry's classmate. Could I talk to Henry?
Alex	:	Sorry friend. At the moment he is not at home. Could I help you?
Sam	:	Thank you. When he comes, inform him that there is going to be held a cricket match at the school ground at 2.30 p.m. So, he should reach there by all means at 2 o'clock.
Alex	:	I'll do that.
Sam	:	Thank you.

Message

Henry,

Your friend Sam told me that there is going to be held a cricket match at the school ground at 2.30 p.m. and that you should be there at 2 o'clock.

Alex

Exercise 1

On the basis of the following telephonic conversation prepare your message.

Johnny	:	Hello! Who's there?
Tina	:	This is Tina, Rita's classmate. Could I talk to her?
Johnny	:	Sorry. At present she is not at home. Is there any message?
Tina	:	Yes. When she comes, tell her that there will be no fancy dress competition tomorrow.
Johnny	:	I'll do that.
Tina	:	Thank you.

Message

____

____

____

____

Exercise 2

On the basis of the following telephonic conversation prepare Diana's message for Lily.

Diana	:	Hello! Who's there?
Annie	:	This is Annie, Lily's classmate. Could I talk to her?
Diana	:	Sorry, she is not at home. Could I convey your message to her?
Annie	:	Oh! How kind of you. When she comes, tell her that I have found out her lost ring and I shall come to give it to her tomorrow in the morning.
Diana	:	I'll do that.
Annie	:	Thank you.

Message

____

____

____

____

Exercise 3

On the basis of the following telephonic conversation write James' message for John.

James	:	Hello! Who's there?
Peter	:	This is Peter, John's friend. Could I talk to John?
James	:	Sorry, he is not at home at the moment.
Peter	:	Oh, I see. Would you please convey my message to him?
James	:	Why not?

Peter	:	Thank you. When he comes, tell him my brother has come from America and has brought a few gifts for John. So, he should come at mine and collect his gifts.
James	:	I'll do that.
Peter	:	Thank you.

Message

____

____

____

____

Exercise 4

On the basis of the following conversation write Lily's message for Roma.

Lily	:	Hello! Who's there?
Dolly	:	This is Dolly, Roma's classmate. Could I talk to Roma?
Lily	:	Sorry, she is not here at the moment. Is there any message?
Dolly	:	Yes. When she comes, tell her there is going to be a special practical class of biology today at 5 p.m. She must not miss it.
Lily	:	I'll do that.
Dolly	:	Thank you.

Message

____

____

____

____

Exercise 5

On the basis of the following conversation write John's message to Mary.

John	:	Hello! Who's there?
Tom	:	This is Tom, Mary's classmate. Could I talk to her?
John	:	Sorry, she has gone to the market. Could I help you?

Tom	:	Thank you. When she comes, tell her that tomorrow she should bring my chemistry book that she borrowed from me a few days ago.
John	:	I'll do that.
Tom	:	Thank you.

Message

____

____

____

____

____

____

____

Diary-Writing

Last Sunday you caught a thief at midnight. Describe the incident in your diary.

Diary-Writing

Last night was a disturbing as well as an adventurous one for me. For some unknown reason, the goddess of sleep was eluding me. I was tossing in my bed. There was not a wink of sleep in my eyes. I was thinking about my friends. How generous all of them were!

I got down the bed to close the window through which the blasts of chilly wind were entering my room. Hardly had I

____

____

____

____

____

____

____

Exercise 6

Last night, you had an interesting dream. Describe it in your diary.

Diary-Writing

Exercise 7

Yesterday, you visited the exhibition. Note down in your diary what special items you saw there.

Diary-Writing

Exercise 8

You have a number of birds in the aviary in your house. Note down in your diary what birds you like the most and why.

Diary-Writing

Notices

Through a notice of about 30 words to be put on the notice board of your school inform the students of your school about the science exhibition that is going to be held shortly in your school.

Notice

Dear students,

All of you will be glad to know that a science exhibition is going to be held in our school within a week. All of you are invited there.

Secretary

Exercise 9

There is going to be a fancy dress competition in your school within a week. Prepare a notice of about 30 words to be put on the notice board of your school inviting all the students there.

Notice

____

____

____

____

Exercise 10

There have been devastating floods in the lower region of Japan. As President of Student Welfare Club, you are to prepare a notice of about 30 words to appeal to the students to contribute their mite to help the victims.

Notice

____

____

____

____

Exercise 11

There is going to be a book fair shortly in your school. Prepare a notice of about 30 words to be put on the notice board of your school, inviting all the students and encouraging them to purchase books in a big way.

Notice

____

____

____

____

Article Writing

You have read an elaborate article in a newspaper describing the importance of non-polluted atmosphere. Now, write an article of the length of a page highlighting the way how to keep our earth pollution free. You may take the help of the following hints.

Hints

- Automobiles and electric gadgets release carbon dioxide and chloroflurocarbon
- Excessive use of pesticides pollute water
- Industrialization pollutes the air
- Nuclear experiments and reactions pollute the air
- Prevention – Grow more plants
- Other suggestions

Article

Pollution is one of the most dangerous problems for man. It does not affect at an individual level only. It affects all kinds of life on earth. For this problem, man himself is responsible. In the wake of living a comfortable life, man is producing more automobiles and electric gadgets which release carbon dioxide and chloroflurocarbon. Both these gases cause green house effect, i.e. they absorb infra red rays of the sun and hence help to increase the global temperature.

Man has polluted not only the air but also the watercourses and oceans through excessive use of pesticides. This has led to toxicity and even depletion of marine life.

Industrialization and nuclear reactions are also responsible for polluting the earth's atmosphere. The best way to get rid of this problem is to grow more plants because the plants release oxygen and take up carbondioxide during photosynthesis. Secondly, man should reduce the production and use of petrol and diesel vehicles. Nuclear experiments should be banned. Existing nuclear weapons should be kept under strict control.

Exercise 12

You have read an elaborate article in a magazine describing the benefits of a morning walk. Write an article highlighting the value of a morning walk.

Hints

- Fresh air, full of oxygen
- Chirping of birds
- Singing of farmers while working in fields
- Dew drops
- Calmness all around
- Other benefits

Article

Postcard Writing

Write a postcard to your friend congratulating him on his grand success in the examination.

POSTCARD

Los Angeles 18th August, 2001 Dear Tony, I congratulate you on your grand success in the Matriculation Examinations and hope that you will repeat your performance even in the next year.	ADDRESS Stamp To Tony Lewis 68, Willington Road California Pin

Exercise 13

Write a postcard to your friend inviting him to your birthday party which is being held on a particular date.

POSTCARD

	ADDRESS Stamp Pin

Exercise 14

Write a postcard to your father asking him for $100 that you want to spend on some important books.

POSTCARD

ADDRESS

Stamp

Pin

Exercise 15

Write a postcard to your uncle thanking him for having sent you a valuable birthday gift.

POSTCARD

ADDRESS

Stamp

Pin

UNIT 26

READING SKILLS

COMPREHENSION - I

I Still Remember the Day

I still remember the day when a man named, Mr Hood was called in a party which was being held in a five star hotel. Mr Hood was a well-known connoisseur of food, and was hailed as "Master Gourmet". After having a spot of every kind of dishes there, he gave his approval that all those were fit for human beings and were tasty too. It was something new for me and probably I was the only Indian in the party. So I heard Mr Hood very attentively, much more attentively than others did. Now, the guests started eating exotic dishes. I was puzzled to see the dishes at my table being unable to decide properly what to start with. At last I dared catch hold of a crisp flat cake with a pattern of squares over it. I was about to bite into it when Mr Hood appeared before me and said, "Gentleman! It is a waffle and is eaten with sweet sauce." A faint smile flitted across his face. I at once made up my mind to get some knowledge about a few dishes. So, I put my plate aside and said to Mr Hood, "What is this?" "Oh, that is croissant. Indeed, it is a small sweet roll and is popular in France." Hardly had Mr Hood finished with his information when I put one more question, "What is this, sir?" "This is a strawberry gateau," he said gently with his eye shut and with a quick sweep of his tongue, he slewed his dry lips. Before I could ask him my next question, he himself started telling me about the other dishes there.

"This is Swiss roll. It is a kind of cake containing jam. Close to your hand, it is a Danish pastry. It is sweet and contains apple, nuts, etc and is covered with icing. On the table behind you, it is a tray of cheese baguettes. These look like sticks; they are crispy outside but soft inside," "Thanks, Mr Hood, for giving me so valuable knowledge about these exotic dishes. "Oh, no mention, please!" said Mr Hood.

Exercise 1

A. On the basis of your reading the above passage, answer the following questions.

1. Who was Mr Hood?

____

2. What is a waffle?

____

3. Why did not the author eat anything in the party?

____

____

4. What is a Swiss roll? How is it different from a bread roll?

____

____

5. Write the names of at least five exotic dishes.

(a) ____

(b) ____

(c) ____

(d) ____

(e) ____

B. Use each of the following pairs of words in the pattern given below.

Gateau —— Swiss roll
Gateau was tasty and Swiss rolls were good too.

1. danish pastries —— cheese baguettes

____

2. apple pies —— jam doughnut

____

3. tairy cake —— waffle

____

4. wedding cake —— sponge cake

____

5. cheese and tomato roll —— croissant

____

C. Use the following phrases and words in sentences of your own.

1. connoisseur of music ____________________.
2. make up one's mind ____________________.
3. indeed ____________________.
4. called in ____________________.
5. sweep of his tongue ____________________.
6. icing ____________________.
7. crispy ____________________.
8. tray of cheese baguettes ____________________.
9. tasty ____________________.
10. catch hold of something ____________________.

D. Tick (✓) the statement which is true and cross (x) the false one.

1. Mr Hood was a man expert on matters involving the judgement of taste of dishes. ( )
2. The author bit into a waffle and stepped forward to confront Mr Hood face to face. ( )
3. A waffle is eaten with lemon juice. ( )
4. A waffle bears squarish marks over it. ( )
5. A danish pastry was placed on the table just behind the author. ( )
6. The author wolfed down a lot of food in the party. ( )
7. A cheese baguette looks like a stick. ( )

COMPREHENSION - II

Of A Particular Brand

Nature lovers of a particular brand have a different kind of mind. Even in secluded areas they manage to get something which provides food to their thought and enables them to feel immense pleasure in things which may seem horrible to others. Once such a nature-lover was passing by a house which was engulfed by fire. It was a God-sent opportunity to the nature-lover for enjoyment. The long tongue-like flames of fire were blazing the surroundings with a dazzling light. Outside the house the street was crawling with gloomy faces and eyes full of tears. All this caught the soul of the nature-lover. He immediately took out his camera and began to shoot. What gave him the never-ending pleasure was the fizzling sound of the burning furniture of the house. After sometime the flames of fire seemed to be cooling down. Obviously, the whole of the furniture had burnt to a cinder. There was nothing more in the house which could burn.

The nature lover shook his head in disappointment. He was watching the end of the best scene of his life. He started crying and pulling his hair. His voice was even louder than that of the owner of the house. Hundreds of people crowded round him. They thought that the man had the softest heart in the world who had real sympathy with those who had suffered. Almost forgetting the owner of the burnt house altogether, the people tried to console him but in vain. Meanwhile, the man had almost gone mad and he even tore down his own shirt in a state of utter anguish and despair. The next day his picture appeared in the newspapers as one of the most genuine lovers of mankind ever born.

Exercise 2

A. On the basis of your reading the above passage, answer the following questions.

1. What kind of person was the nature-lover?

____

____

2. Describe the incident which made the nature-lover enjoy himself even in an unpleasant situation?

____

____

____

____

____

3. What was the fizzling sound which pleased the nature-lover so much?

____

____

4. Why did a number of people try to console the nature-lover?

____

____

B. Use each of the following pairs of words in the pattern given below.

cake —— tea

The cake was stale and tea was bad either.

1. fruits —— vegetables

____

2. jam —— pastries

____

3. ice-cream —— drinks

____

4. coffee —— snacks

____

5. biscuits —— cookies

____

C. What does/do the underlined word/words in each sentence mean? Select the meaning strictly in accordance with the passage given and write down 'a' or 'b' in brackets, whichever is correct.

1. Even in a <u>secluded</u> area the particular kinds of nature-lovers can manage to find something pleasuresome.
   (a) remote area
   (b) bustling area ( )

2. Such a nature-lover can feel <u>immense</u> pleasure in anything.
   (a) a lot of
   (b) a bit of ( )

3. The street was <u>crawling with</u> gloomy faces.
   (a) full of
   (b) lacking in ( )

4. <u>Obviously</u> the whole of the furniture had burnt to a cinder.
   (a) plainly
   (b) unknowingly ( )

5. A dazzling light
   (a) a dull light
   (b) a bright light ( )

6. Hundreds of people crowded round him
   (a) came around him
   (b) caught him ( )

D. Tick (✓) the correct part of speech of the underlined word used in each set.

1. Once a nature-lover was passing by a house.
   (a) adjective (b) adverb (c) noun
2. The nature-lover immediately took out his camera and began to shoot.
   (a) infinitive (b) gerund (c) reflexive pronoun
3. The street was crawling with gloomy faces.
   (a) preposition (b) adverb (c) conjunction
4. The clouds of smoke were emerging from the nearby house.
   (a) pronoun (b) adjective (c) noun
5. Obviously, the whole of furniture had burnt to a cinder.
   (a) pronoun (b) adjective (c) noun

COMPREHENSION - III

The Indian Farmer

An Indian farmer is known as the second God because he produces different kinds of food stuffs for us. An Indian farmer, particularly the one who has only a small holding, is a poor, abject creature. No doubt, the financial condition of the big farmers has become better than it was a few years back. The small farmers are often under heavy debt which they are unable to pay back. Being illiterate, a marginal farmer is normally unable to handle the situation through which he is passing. He keeps incurring loans all his life to get his daughter married or to get his addicted son educated and soon many of such farmers themselves, too fall victims to bad habit like drinking and drug-taking. In this way, they go on becoming poorer and poorer. Some of them have to commit suicide being unable to pay back their debts. The Government is trying its best to save them from this devastating situation by providing them free water and electricity and also by giving them loans at low interest rates. But according to them the small farmers are unable to make hay while the sun shines because they have no tubewells of their own to avail themselves of these opportunities. So, they have to buy water from the big farmers. Thus, one of the important sections of our country has been forced circumstances to wallow in abject poverty.

Exercise 3

A. On the basis of your reading the above passage, answer the following questions.

1. Describe the financial condition of small peasants in our country.

____

____

2. What are the key factors which do not allow a small farmer to become rich?

____

____

3. Can you suggest some modes to improve the financial condition of small farmers?

____

____

4. What are the occasions when a small farmer often takes loans in a big way?

____

____

B. Use the following words in sentences of your own.

1. still ______________________________.
2. provide ______________________________.
3. loans ______________________________.
4. financial ______________________________.
5. produce ______________________________.
6. wallow ______________________________.
7. addicted ______________________________.
8. adject ______________________________.
9. avail ______________________________.
10. illiterate ______________________________.

C. Complete the following sentences.

1. A farmer's job is to produce ____________________

____

2. Usually small farmers are illiterate and ____________________

____

3. The farmer with a small piece of land has to face a number of difficulties such as

____

4. Some of the factors __________ are making the small farmers poorer and poorer are ____________________.

5. The government is also trying to uplift the small farmers by ____________________

____

D. Replace the underlined word in each of the following sentences with the word conveying the opposite meaning and rewrite each of the sentences. The first one has been done for you.

1. An Indian farmer is a <u>poor</u> creature.
   An Indian farmer is a rich creature.

2. The small farmers are mostly <u>debtors</u>.

____

3. Being <u>illiterate</u> they are <u>unable</u> to handle the situation.

____

4. The government supplies them electricity at a <u>cheaper</u> rate.

____

5. A <u>small</u> farmer is forced by circumstances to go for loans.

____

E. Circle the word in each set which does not rhyme with the other two.

1.	indian	russian	germany
2.	evident	valiant	different

3.	elite	delight	bright
4.	better	matter	bazaar
5.	afraid	broad	parade
6.	watch	wasp	ball
7.	financial	providential	conditional
8.	mean	vision	lean

COMPREHENSION-IV

Newspaper

It is a fact that a newspaper is the true voice of man. It gives us information from every corner of the world about different fields like sports, politics, stock market, science, history and so on. A newspaper is divided into different columns such as matrimonial, advertisements, columns for women, children, old people, etc. One can make one's voice heard by the higher authorities through the newspapers by sending one's views which are then placed in the Readers' Column. Through the newspapers even a common man can rebuke the government or give his views that may differ from that of the government. Newspapers also keep us in touch with the current affairs as well as historic findings and researches. Reading a newspaper early in the morning has become our habit and we cannot do without it at any cost. We get a lot of knowledge about the fluctuating economic situation of our country and also that of the world in general. Thus, newspapers do not give us just the news, they also give us views of different groups and individuals on various topics besides so many other things.

Exercise 4

A. On the basis of your reading the above passage, answer the following question.

1. What is the importance of newspapers?

 ____

 ____

2. Give one such factor which helps to prove that newspapers are the true voice of man.

 ____

 ____

3. Name a few common newspaper columns.

____

____

4. Why can't we do without a newspaper?

____

____

B. Give synonyms of the following.

1. rebuke ____________________.
2. occurred ____________________.
3. knowledge ____________________.
4. unspoken ____________________.
5. efficiency ____________________.

C. Give antonyms of the following.

1. pleased ____________________.
2. prosperous ____________________.
3. different ____________________.
4. true ____________________.
5. divide ____________________.

D. Complete the following sentences.

1. Through newspapers we get knowledge about ____________________

____

2. Newspapers also keep us in touch with ____________________

____

3. A newspaper works as a bridge between higher authorities and ____________

____

4. Through newspapers even a common man can ______________________________

____

5. A newspaper is the voice of ______________________________________

____

COMPREHENSION - V

Health is Wealth

"Health is wealth" is a true saying. A man with sound body can do a lot of work in this competitive world. Only healthy people are selected for government jobs. So, a man with good physique even if poor, can fare better in life than a wealthy but sick person. A healthy man will always be self-dependent while a wealthy person may or may not be so. Wealth cannot bring health. But health can bring wealth. A healthy person may not be very rich but he is a pride for the country. On the other hand, a wealthy person with ill-health is a liability to the nation, as he has to remain busy to get himself cured of various ailments most of the time in his life and thus, he can do little for the country. In fact, he is unable to do anything worthwhile for the country even when he has a genuine desire in his heart for doing so. But on the other hand, a healthy person can do anything in different fields that can bring prosperity to the country.

Exercise 5

A. On the basis of your reading the above passage answer the following questions.

1. Draw a comparison between a poor but healthy and a wealthy but ill person.

____

____

2. Give support to the slogan. "Health brings wealth" by writing a few lines.

____

____

3. Can you suggest some ways to keep healthy?

____

____

B. Tick (✓) the correct part of speech of the underlined word in each set.

1. A man with a sound body can do even tough jobs.
   (a) noun (b) adverb (c) adjective

2. A healthy man can also be selfdependent.
   (a) noun (b) verb (c) adjective

3. Riches are not the symbol of health.
   (a) noun (b) adverb (c) interjection

4. A healthy person is a symbol of prosperity.
   (a) adjective (b) verb (c) noun

5. A chronically ill person remains busy to get himself cured of diseases.
   (a) verb (b) adjective (c) adverb

C. Give synonyms of the following words.

1. ill ______________________.
2. healthy ______________________.
3. wealthy ______________________.
4. busy ______________________.
5. bring ______________________.

D. Give antonyms of the following.

1. cure ______________________.
2. rich ______________________.
3. better ______________________.
4. desire ______________________.
5. great ______________________.

E. Complete the following sentences.

1. Health is ____.
2. A healthy man is always ______________________________________.

3. A nation will prefer a healthy person to a wealthy one because ______________________

____.

4. Achieving joy in different fields is easy for ______________________ because

____.

COMPREHENSION - V

Read the passage carefully.

The consequence of the combination of overeating and physical inactivity is obesity. The extent to which obesity can adversely affect the health and well-being of a person is best exemplified by the modern day Nauruans, a small nation of 7000 once-happy-and-healthy people of a tiny, 20-square-kilometre island country of Nauru in the Western Pacific.

Their small island was an equatorial paradise with lush green forests and waters full of fish. It had enough for everyone. Unfortunalely, they suddenly found themselves rich beyond belief. Huge deposits of high-grade phosphate had been sighted in the island in the 19th century. In the past three decades, since independence, they have recklessly mined their country for phosphate for export and converted their beautiful country into a barren uninhabitable land.

With the money pouring in millions of dollars, they imported an incredible number of cars, gadgets and junk food for easy and luxurious living and human labour to work for them. With plenty to eat and no work to do, the nation of active healthy people have converted themselves into sick and lethargic, fat and flabby men and women, many of whom weigh over 135 kilograms.

It is frightening but true that over 50 per cent of the population has become diabetic, and there is rampant hypertension and heart disease, cutting short their life-span to an average of only 55 years. Now that the phosphate deposits have all but disappeared, their country converted into a barren wasteland and money no longer pouring in, it is not difficult to imagine their fate.

Though less glaring, the story of neoaffluent families in other countries, including India, is not very different. Quick prosperity with physical intertia is a risky proposition.

Exercise 6

A. On the basis of reading the above passage answer the questions that follow. Write complete sentences.

1. Give two causes of obesity.

   Two causes of obesity are

   a. ______________________________________

   b. ______________________________________

2. What is the total population of Nauru?

____

3. What was the discovery that changed the life of the Nauruans?

____

4. How has Nauru changed into a barren land?

____

5. What kind of a "paradise" was Nauru before the discovery?

____

6. What change came in the life-style of the Nauruans?

____

____

B. Name four diseases and abnormalities from which the present day Nauruans suffer.

The present day Nauruans suffer from —

a. ____

b. ____

c. ____

d. ____

C. There is another word for "inactivity" mentioned in the passage. Identify the word.

Another word for "inactivity" as mentioned in the passage is ____________

D. Give antonyms of :

a. Barren

b. Risky

____

____

UNIT 27

WRITING SKILLS

ESSAY WRITING

Friends or Foe

"Friend in need is a friend indeed" is the definition of true friend. All of us have friends of different kinds. Some are similar to us, while others are quite different. When asking which kind I like, I will choose the latter one.

Let us see the advantages of both kinds first. Friends who are similar to us can fully understand us. They may think the way as we do. Suppose your boss blamed you, but you did not think it was your fault. A similar friend may advise you to explain the fact to your boss while a different one is likely to suggest that you just pass it by. Which one is more acceptable? To me, one who always sticks to facts, explaining it is the only way I can get released.

Every coin has two sides, as saying goes. There are many good aspects of different friends which cannot be surpassed. Friends of different kind challenge you and they can make your life full of adventures. They can broaden your mind. I have a friend who works as a tour guide. He has traveled to many places in the world. After each trip, he will talk to me and give me much information about the culture and lives of the people who live there. To me, a student who has not enough money or time to travel in myself, such information is valuable. In addition, when I need a second opinion, I will turn to different friends. They may think of different aspects of the problem while a similar friend can only consider it as I myself do.

In summary, my propensity is for different friends. I am a shy person who cannot come across many things in my life, so I need friends who are different from me. Tomorrow is another day, said in the novel "Gone with the Wind". I want my tomorrow to be different from today, and my life more colorful.

True Power of Meditation

The way we look at the life is not exactly the real life. It is only the superficial layer of the mind which is controlling our senses with predefined limitations, thereby creating a illusion, which we are forced to believe it as life. If we analyse our mind, we will be surprised to notice that not even ten percent of our mind is utilised towards meeting daily requirements of our day to day life. That is to say, major portion of brain remains under utilised throughout our life. The art of utilization of this untapped power of our brain which gives you ultimate happiness and satisfaction is meditation in real sense.

It is not the race, nationality, colour of skin, financial assets and such other many millions of superficial trademarks that govern our lives in this mortal world. We accuse and scold each other in an attempt to gain a pseudo edge over other and to satisfy our EGO. But in the bargain we loose out most precious and sacred aspect of life that is peace and satisfaction. Let me give you an example technically/ scientifically. Any electronic, electrical, mechanical or biological device is supposed to be performing to its optimal efficiency if there is little or minimal element of heat dissipation involved. Though there are ways and means to put a heat sink in place to save the device from damage due to such dissipation, yet it cannot be ruled out completely (Theoretically yes but practically no). Thus the life of device/ gadget is completely dependent on this prime factor which always exists and is inversely proportional to each other.

Same way life of a human being (device) and Anger/ Fear/ Dissatisfaction (Heat dissipation) etc are inversely proportional to each other. The more you dissipate, the more you are susceptible to fast decay (and ultimately death which is a plain truth).

Thus, pointing finger on each other will not lead you any where. It will only make you more vulnerable to claws of death. Please answer me, can anyone conquer this ultimate reality that is death just because he / she is fairer than other or living in a developed country? Mind you no one is inferior to other. It is only the time, place and cause that govern and combination of all may lead us to the destiny.

Everyone has a subtle energy present inside. When we get connected ourselves to pervading cosmic power through meditation, we tend to overcome all our ills and egos thereby reach a state of mind/body/soul of immense happiness and peace, I was talking earlier.

Most of you might have guessed it correct. If not then I tell you it is Yoga. It is amalgamation of all existing religions and Gods and their preaching. I love my country and am proud of the same very much as you all are for your respective countries. But have you understood yourself completely? If No, then please learn to live without heat dissipation and overcome the same by power resting inside you.

Let me tell you about an experienced Engineer looking for job as a second career. But after nearly thousand of applications and equal number of no from employers, he feels stronger and powerful and continues to do the same in months to come. He now really care for people, who are dissatisfied, frustrated and Egoist educated lot with superiority stigma attached to them as cancerous growth, which often get attracted to super magnet "death" faster than usual.

Life in a Big City

Life in a big city is a mixed bag. It is a heaven to some and a hell to others. Those who have money and resources enough to live in a decent air-conditioned house and own a comfortable, luxurious air-conditioned car to move from one place to the other, are indeed, the blessed ones. They must have done a lot of good deeds in their previous life, as the old superstitious people will tell you. And this absolves them from all the wrongs they may be doing now in this life through cheating, swindling and smuggling and by spreading pollution, if nothing else, by vainly roving in their vehicles through the streets and on the roads to carry out their murky, nefarious multi-pronged activities. Yes, a big city is a haven for all kinds of anti-social elements.

This, however, is only one side of the picture. Most of the people living in a big city are highly responsible persons. But the most miserable is the condition of the poor slum and shanty dwellers. Day and night, they are surrounded by dirt and squalor in their narrow hole-like dwellings and they hardly make both ends meet while sweating with arduous labour from dawn till late at night.

The condition of the common middle and lower middle-class people is not much better. Among the great problems they have to face are the problems of suitable housing, erratic bus service, pollution, education of children, expensive health aids and the like.

Quite a big chunk of people living in a big city is virtually unemployed or only semi-employed. Most of these people have come from distant places in search of greener pastures and stayed put as their never-ending search continues. Still, they feel more satisfied here as they are able to find at least petty, odd jobs on meagre wages here which at their home places in villages and small towns they are unable to get.

Proverbially, life in a big city is very tiring. But it has its plus points too. It is the place where we can have avenues for employment in offices and business concerns and opportunities for education in universities, schools, colleges and academies. Here we have big libraries, museums and art galleries where we can enhance our knowledge in different fields. Ultra-modern health facilities and aids are available at first class hospitals in big cities only. No doubt, distances are long, but even if one does not have one's own conveyance, one can get taxis and auto-rickshaws besides buses and trains round the clock. Traffic jams are certainly a drawback but such minor hassles have to be tolerated in view of overall plus points.

There are several means of entertainment in a big city. There are so many historical places and tourist spots which one can visit. Then there are theatres, cinema halls and auditoriums there. Several entertaining programmes such as circus shows, magic shows and exhibitions are always going on in one or the other part of a big city. Those who have a sociable nature can join clubs or attend lectures, seminars and workshops. Thus life in a big city is tiring or boring only for those who lack sociability. If one would like to be alone, one can attend a yoga camp or simply visit some park or gym or slimming centre.

Even the highly religious minded people have a good place in big city where there are so many temples and other religious places of all kinds of sects and communities. Besides, there are religious souls galore in a big city whose religious programmes and gospels anybody can attend with profit if he has the genuine inclination for such things.

For children, there are often good parks even in some not very big cities. But in metropolises, they have the facility to visit the Zoological Peak or Dolls' Museum.

So, there is fare for all in a big city except for the poorest who find themselves being ground under the unbearable weight of high prices of essential commodities and otherwise high cost of living.

Life Story of A Mango Tree

The significance of trees for all kinds of life on this planet is well-known and, so, I'm not going to explain it. Moreover, self-praise is no better than self-pity and I detest either.

I vaguely remember that many years ago I was just a seed. It does not need to be explained how human beings mercilessly throw away seeds after eating mangoes which they, I should say, suck to the bone. That only speaks of the deliciousness of the mango fruit, my father, and is an indirect compliment to him.

I was one of the lucky seeds selected by a celebrated horticulturist for sowing in his magnificent orchard. I was even luckier than other seeds in getting a particular place for cultivation where air and light were available in abundance.

Before sowing me, the horticulturist's gardener soaked me in water for some time. Then he dug up the earth and mixed some compost in it. He dug a hole and buried me a few centimetre below the surface and then covered the soil which was already moist. However, he watered the surrounding of the place where he had buried me.

After a few days, I sprouted. My roots began to spread below in the soil as I sent a shoot upwards outside the soil. Not much later, the shoot spread into green and purple leaflets with a stem. I looked very innocent and attractive, indeed. The gardener knew the children's irresistible longing for such colourful plantlets and he specifically guarded me against any danger. He watered me regularly and applied fertilizers and also kept me safe from dangers such as those of scorching rays of the sun, hail, storm, and excessive rain.

I continued growing to the great delight of the gardener who visited me daily and the horticulturist whose visits, no doubt, were few and far between but were always full of affection and approbation for me. The gardener too got accolade from him for having taken so good care of me.

As a number of years elapsed, I grew up into a big tree as I am now. I have a tall trunk, numerous branches and innumerable green leaves spreading like a canopy. I welcome rain and tolerate heat, cold and hail. I find kinship within cool breeze and passing clouds who I feel convey some message to me. Birds come and perch on my branches and sing melodious songs. I'm, in particular, the haunt of some singing birds such as nightingales and cuckoos. I offer the most hilarious sanctuary to the peacocks who find great solace under my branches and raise their sweet voices in mirth as they dance, rhythmically spreading their colourful wings.

I'm extremely useful to human beings, only if they'd like to realize. I give them shade and make them enjoy my beauty. This season, as the flowers on my branches have changed into tiny buds, the latter will within a few months grow into fruit which will first be green in raw form and will become golden yellow as it ripens. In raw form, the fruit may be cut and used as pickle by adding spices and mustard oil to it. But my real taste will be relished by one and all as I'm allowed to ripen as fruit. I call myself a tree as well as a fruit. So, I have the same name in either case.

When I was a seed, the fruit was my father, but now when I'm a tree, the fruit may be regarded as my issue and this is, indeed, a strange phenomenon. Isn't it?

I won't mind if I'm eaten as fruit as I'll bear more and more fruit from year to year, and, moreover, as fruit, I've the quality of growing again into another tree if proper care is provided to me. But what I fear most is the axe in the hands of man that hangs over me like the sword of Damocles. It is, indeed, very unfortunate that man should be so greedy to grab all land area and use it for construction work. I fear that some day the horticulturist may sell this orchard where I live most happily with so many other mango and other trees. The purchaser might axe me with other trees, level the ground and thus make the end of me. I realize that my fear is genuine and I pray that some sincere environmentalist and genuine lover of plants should step in to save my life and that of my sister plants. Let him explain to the avaricious land-grabbers and sky-scraper-lovers that plants are essential as they absorb carbon dioxide gas from air and release oxygen, thus maintaining balance between the two gases in the atmosphere. And this is how plants ensure, protect and maintain all life on earth. I'm happy that I have got the opportunity to serve all earthly beings through self-sacrifice, self-negation and dedication, but I should be allowed to continue my mission. This is what I plead with all the well-meaning human beings on the planet.

PARAGRAPH WRITING

Environmental Pollution

Pollution is the bane of modern society. It is the scourge which is responsible for untold misery to modern man. It affects man's health adversely when he consumes polluted air, water and food. To a great extent, the problem is man's own creation. When man manipulates with the course of nature, the nemesis is unavoidable. Nature gives man the vast invaluable treasure of lush green forests. Man cuts down the trees for his own selfish purpose and thus causes decrease of the ratio of oxygen in the atmosphere. Pollution in the air is also caused by innumerable vehicles plying on the roads and emitting obnoxious petrol and diesel fumes. Thousands of big and small factories also give out clouds of pernicious carbon-laden smoke and make life a hell for the people, particularly the children. These factories also release lethal chemicals in the water channels which cause the death of aquatic life on a large-scale. The excessive use of pesticides and insecticides pollutes the soil. Nuclear experiments, perfumes and gases used in refrigerators and air-conditioners also bring about the green-house effect. Thus, if man has to survive on this planet, he must pay more attention to avoiding environmental pollution, including noise pollution. Otherwise, his existence on the earth may be in danger.

A Rainy Day in Summer

It was Monday morning and the day was as hot as the previous one. I was sitting by the window and looking out at the people going here and there with their clothes wet with perspiration. Suddenly, I saw massive smoke-coloured clouds hovering the sky. And I went happier when their gurgling sound approached my ears. I prayed to God for the rain to come. In a minute, the sky went noisy with thunder and it blazed with the zigzag lightning. A cool breeze began to blow. After some-time, it began to drizzle outside which changed into light rain. In a few minutes, it changed into a torrential rain. I was overjoyed as I heard clattering sound of the rain-drops. Within no time the drains of streets went flooded. Not only the children but also a few zingy youths came out on the streets and roads to welcome the first shower of that season. The roads were still busy, as the people were going to their offices, factories or other business places under their umbrellas. The paper-boats were sailing all around in the street. The jolly adolescents had made the atmosphere more charming by singing filmy songs. When the rain stopped, I came out of my house to get a view of the world around me. I found the world really charming as the sky was garlanded with a huge rainbow. Every tree and building looked as though it had been brushed with new colours. The birds were chirping merrily in the trees. In short the whole world looked adorned like a bride.

Our School Peon

I read in one of the most expensive schools in Delhi. A great strength of the boys and girls is being taught here by highly learned teachers. There are four peons in our school. All of them are poor but well-mannered. Peter is one of them. He is an orphan, who was brought up by the warden of an orphanage. He did his matriculation in a government school. Now-a-days, he is living in the campus of our school. He leads an extremely simple life. He never wears costly dresses. But he wears clean and well-ironed shirt and trousers. He respects and obeys the teachers and he also conveys the messages to them from the Principal. Sometimes, he has to ring the bell. During sports days, he has to wash the floors of the school and also has to do the dusting of furniture of the school. He brings water and eatables for the teachers and non-teaching staff, whenever he is ordered to do so. Peter is a regular and punctual man. He is married and has two sons, who are getting their education in a government school. He lives from hand to mouth, as his salary is small. He loves all the students and talks to them in a polite manner. All the students like him very much.

Price Rise

The prices of consumer goods are on the rise in our country. It depends upon the production and consumption of the things. Since India is a densely populated country, the consumption of essential commodities is always on a high scale, while the production of such things as tea, sugar, wheat, cereals, vegetables, etc. is a game of luck, as we are mostly dependent on the weather-god for the production of these items. It is a matter of pride for us, the Indians, that our country is one of the most important producers of wheat, tea and milk across the world. But the huge population of this country spoils the game. We have also to spend a lot of foreign exchange to import the petroleum products. And a slight upswing in their rates in the international market, hits our country's economy badly. In such times our government is forced by the unfavourable circumstances to increase the freight and this hits every section of our country. Whenever an item runs short in our country, the black-marketers have a heyday as they sell the same at substantially higher rates. The Indian government should ban all petrol and diesel-based vehicles in this poor country except where they are absolutely necessary. The petrol and diesel should be supplied only to the defence, agriculture and industry. And government should pass strict laws against such black marketers. Strikes and lock-outs should be banned. All out efforts should be made to increase production and decrease luxurious expenditure and avoid waste.

LETTER WRITING

A. Writing a Resume, Bio-data or Curriculum Vitae (CV)

Name : ______________________________.

Address : ______________________________.

Nationality : ______________________________.

Date of birth : ______________________________.

Marital status : ______________________________.

Educational and
other Qualifications : ______________________________

____

____

____.

Skills/extracurricular
activities : ______________________________

____

____.

Present employment,
if any : ______________________________

____

____.

Exercise 1

1. Give the CV of a young man, John Adam, who has done MCA from IGNOU.
2. Give the CV of a young girl who has done NTT from an institute.

B. Write a letter to your friend who couldn't get any prize in a debate.

12 Regal Estates
Hong Kong

16 October 20...

My dear Simon

I was not shocked but only pained when I heard the judgement delivered by the worthy judges. I'm talking of debate.

What pained me was your failure to get a single prize. But, frankly speaking, I do not blame the judges. Their judgement was right, and that is why I was not shocked.

I, being your sincere friend and your well-wisher, would advise you not to take my words ill. I must convey to you, and I think you must yourself have realized, your performance at the debate was least laudable. You could not cut convincingly a single argument forwarded by your rival. Moreover, you faltered and stuttered frequently, and what was most damaging, you spoke abruptly without caring for the arguments put forward by your adversary and even interrupted her when she hadn't yet finished her speech.

I think, this dismal failure of yours is a blessing in disguise. It will prove for you a stepping stone for future successes as you are now bound to work hard and be more diligent and cautious. Had the judges given you a prize, they would have been blamed for partiality, and rightly so, and that would have marred your career, since you would have got swelled up with complacency and false pride.

I hope once again you won't take my words in a different light. Please convey my regards to your revered parents.

Yours sincerely

(Sophia)

C. Write a letter to your father who has gone abroad, giving him home news.

69 Rose Avenue
Bangkok

15 July 20...

My dear Father

We were all overjoyed when we read in your recent letter about the progress you have made in your business trip abroad. Moreover, Tony and I were overwhelmed when we studied the French and Swiss stamps you sent us with your letter. What impressed us most, and that particularly from the description of the various stamps in your letter, was the genuine regard the foreigners have for all kinds of flora and fauna, while we at home merely cry from housetops, highlighting our hollow love and mercy for poor animals, birds and plants.

One bad news. Tony has failed in the JET. Lest you should feel despondent, papa, I hasten to add that he has been selected by Roche for field work at ten thousand per month. This has been possible due to his superb performance at the interview held last week.

As far as I'm concerned, my studies are going on smoothly. I've won a special prize in a swimming competition. As for histrionics in the youth festival, I couldn't quite come up to the mark. But I don't feel there's any occasion for lament, as I now quite understand that successes and failures are part of life.

Mamma? O, she is going to office regularly and I must say to her credit that she has put to shame many stalwarts in her office.

Papa, I've learnt that it is very cold in Sweden even in summer. I hope I needn't advise you to take care of your health. You know it better. Last year you caught pneumonia and this fear haunts me. I hope this will not happen again.

Lots of love, my dear, dear papa. Tony and mamma too are worried and miss you every moment. I hope you are returning soon.

Your loving daughter

(Lolita)

D. Write an application to a company for a job.

28 South Avenue
Paris
.... Date

M/s Warner and Warner
5 Kingston Road
London SE 11 DE

Dear Sirs

Through this communication I hereby apply for the post of an assistant manager, lying vacant in your company. I have come to know about the job through some reliable sources. Please find enclosed a copy of my CV.

I would like to focus your attention towards my qualifications and my specialization in hotel management and I'm sure it would meet your demands.

I am a dynamic young man and I believe in hard work. I am sure I would prove a boon to your company. I have developed a good communication skill. I can speak both French and English equally well.

I look forward to hearing from you.

Yours faithfully

Signature ________________

Name ____________________

Encl: CV (one pg)

E. Write a letter to the editor of a newspaper expressing your views over mindless cutting down of trees.

The Editor
The Times
Nairobi

Date...........

Dear Sir

Should the mindless cutting of trees be called an act of ignorance or cruelty? Needless to describe how vegetation is useful to man. If there were no plants, there would be no oxygen left in the atmosphere which would spell the death-knell for mankind.

Devastating floods in certain regions and acute droughts in others due to absence of forests are some of the living examples of the reaction of nature against man's cruelty. The stuffiness and suffocation in metropolises is brought about on account of the unbearable pollution in the air. And this deficiency can be made up only by growing a large number of plants in and around these cities. We all know that there is no source better than this for increasing the amount of oxygen in the air.

Apart from the efforts of the government agencies, the NGOs should come forward in a big way to grow more plants and bring awareness among the common people to do so on a large-scale.

Yours truly

Andy Robert

F. Write a letter to the President, Municipal Committee of your town requesting him/her to arrange for the construction of a municipal park for children in your locality.

23 Crecent Road
Paris
25 June 20...

The President
Municipal Committee
Paris

Dear Madam

Sub: Construction of a Municipal Park for Children

The area in which I live is a part of our Colony. In common parlance, it is regarded as a posh area. But, most surprisingly, there is not a single park for children in the whole locality.

In the absence of a municipal park, the children have to play on the traffic-ridden roads and in busy streets. Thus, the life of these innocent angels is always in danger. Sometimes, there are bickerings and even scuffles between housewives when the windowpanes of the house of any one of them get broken due to the ball thrown by the helpless playing children.

You are, therefore, requested to arrange for the construction of a municipal park for children in this locality at your earliest.

Thank You

Yours faithfully
(Willam)

Exercise 2

1. Write a letter to your friend, inviting him to a tea party you are giving in a restaurant.
2. Write a letter to your friend describing the excursion you have just been to.
3. Write a letter to the Editor of a daily newspaper complaining about the frequent breakdowns of water supply in your colony.
4. Write a letter to the Post Master to arrange relevant enquiries about the lost Money Order, which was sent to you a month back.
5. Write a letter to the Editor of a newspaper expressing your views on environmental pollution.
6. You have left your old school and gone to join another in some other town. Write a letter to your friend about your new school and tell him how you miss him in the new town.

UNIT 28

Writing, Describing and Making

WRITING A STORY

Please read the following lines and using them, complete the story.

Last night, I was reading a book: "The Wild Beasts".

Last night, I was reading a book: "The Wild Beasts". The book was so interesting that I could not put it down till midnight, in fact, till drowsiness overtook me.

I was only half-asleep when I heard a scratching sound outside. I thought that it must be the rustling of leaves of plants in the lawn as it was blowing hard and the plants were shaking violently like shaky ghosts as I could watch through the gaps in the curtains on the window-panes.

There was a repetition of the scratching sound and it continued for quite a few minutes. I realized that some creature was scratching the door of my room. I was suddenly overtaken by a horrible fear. The idea that some wild beast might have escaped from the zoo and made its way to my room began to haunt my mind.

I heard the scratching sound the third time. One part of my mind wanted me to open the door. But I could not muster courage enough for this. Then along with the whistling sound of the sharp wind and that of the scratching sound on the door of my room, I heard the sound of low moans and growls. The picture of the ferocious black bear about whom I had read in the animal book suddenly appeared in my mind. A sudden shrill cry came out of my lips almost involuntarily.

As my father in the adjoining room heard my loud shriek, he rushed to my room. He found me gasping and trembling with fear. With great difficulty and in a stammering voice I told him what the matter was.

My father looked through the hole in the door and began to smile. Without a moment's hesitation, he opened the door. What did he see? To my great surprise and delight we found a shivering puppy moaning and growling. Meanwhile, my mother had also come. She took the puppy, gave some hot milk to it and wrapped it in a warm blanket. Today the puppy is quite hale and hearty, as it bounces merrily and I also do likewise on seeing it in such a jovial mood. I had long been demanding of my papa and mamma to buy me a charming puppy. And here it was, a God-given gift. Though previously, they had been postponing the matter, they could do nothing now but accept the puppy with a light heart.

Exercise 1

Complete the following Stories starting with the sentences as given.

1. Early in the morning, as I was having a walk in the garden..............
2. Last Sunday, as I was bathing in the canal outside my village..........
3. As the train suddenly came to a halt....................
4. At first it surprised me why Tomy was barking so wildly. As I looked out through the window.........

ARTICLE WRITING

*Write an Article on "**Adulteration of Milk**."*

Everybody has heard about rampant adulteration in food articles such as spices, tea leaves, sugar, gram powder (besan), ghee, etc. People have also heard of the mixing of water in milk. But the manufacturing of chemical milk is a new phenomenon.

If scientific development alone were to be the criterion, the man who invented the manufacturing of chemical milk should deserve some big prize. But the difficulty is that the ingredients which go to make this milk are highly pernicious to health and dangerous. Some of these ingredients are urea, caustic soda, varnish, refined oil, detergents, etc.

Previously, mothers took pride and happiness in administering cow's or buffalo's milk to their loving kids. Now, they do so with trembling hands as they are not sure whether the milk is pure, and if it is adulterated, to what extent it is so.

It is said that chemical milk causes a number of ailments such as cancer, heart trouble, nervous debility, liver disorder, kidney failure, etc. It is a pity that nobody is paying any attention to this menace which is likely to impair the growth of the children of the present and the coming generations. It is even more deplorable that some men at high places are said to be encouraging this practice.

This problem needs to be addressed urgently. Efficient testing centres, manned by competent men and women of integrity should be set up in all towns and cities and at rural centres. The culprits should be dealt with severely. An awakening campaign should be started among the masses through mass media.

Seminars, workshops and public debates should also be held to discuss and highlight this problem. Students and young men and women should be encouraged to participate in the campaign in a big way.

Exercise 2

Write Articles on the following topics.

1. Environmental Pollution
2. Drug Addiction
3. Hazards of Smoking
4. Public Drinking — a Nuisance
5. Rash Driving

REPORTING

Example

You are a reporter for Local News of your town. You witnessed a road accident. Please report the accident to your newspaper.

Two Killed Three Injured In Road Accident

Los Angeles August 13

There was a head-on collision today morning at the Grand Trunk Road between a military jeep and a private car. The driver of the car who was dead drunk was killed on the spot. The jeep driver died while being taken to the local Civil Hospital.

Three other car travelers were seriously injured and are struggling for life in the hospital.

Exercise 3

Change the following headlines into full reports for a newspaper.

1. Hailstorm Destroys Bumper Crops
2. Earthquake Causes Widespread Losses
3. Notorious Criminal Released on Parole
4. Fake Currency Found in Suit Case, Two Held
5. Notorious Gangster Dies in Police Encounter
6. Capital in Grip of Dengue

ITINERARY PLANNING

Examples

You as Head Girl have been asked to plan an itinerary for the Chief Guest on the occasion of Annual Prize Distribution in your school. Please do.

ITINERARY PLANNING

830	Arrival and Reception by the Principal, teachers and student representatives at the school gate.
0835	Tea with Principal in his office.
0915	Departure for the Auditorium - flanked by Principal and Vice Principal.
0920	Standing ovation in the Auditorium.
0925	Welcome Address by the Head Boy.
0930-1130	Function including giving away of prizes.
1130	Cultural show conducted by the students.
1240	Annual Report by the Principal.
0100	Chief Guest's speech.
0115	Thanksgiving by the President, School Managing Committee.
0120	Tea with President, Principal, staff and student representatives in the school canteen.
0150	Departure.

Exercise 4

Write the Itinerary for the following.

1. The Chief Guest on the occasion of Sports Day.
2. The District Inspector of Schools on his visit to your school.
3. The Team of Doctors led by the Civil Surgeon on the occasion of a Blood Bank Camp in your school.
4. The Minister/Governor, etc. on the occasion of inauguration of stadium in your school.

PAMPHLET/POSTER WRITING

Example

Write a Pamphlet/Poster for a Boutique.

MARIGOLD BOUTIQUE

16 ROSE AVENUE, SINGAPORE

SPECIAL

NEW YEAR

OFFER

Get Free Gift with every suit stitched from 1st Jan. to 12th Jan.

Exclusive Suits and Dresses for Ladies

Exclusive Girls Tops

Exclusive Kids Wear

- Bed Covers
- Mats and Carpets
- Night Wear
- Kids Wear
- Curtains
- Purses
- Jeans and Skirts
- School Uniforms

Reasonable Rates Quality Goods

Exercise 5

Write a Pamphlet/Poster for the following.

1. A Departmental Store
2. An Artificial Jewellery Shop
3. A Toy Shop
4. A Book Shop
5. A Restaurant
6. An Art Gallery
7. A Museum
8. A Circus Show
9. A Magic Show
10. A Beauty Parlour

MAGIC TIME EXPERIMENTING FOR FUN

Example

Show one funny experiment.

- o Ask your friend to sit in a revolving chair.
- o Let him stretch both of his arms forward out of the chair as far as possible.
- o Revolve the chair violently.
- o Let him bring his arms immediately inside the chair.

Observation:

The revolving speed of the chair increases slightly though for a moment or so, instead of decreasing which later happens slowly.

Conclusion:

It is a matter of earth's gravitational pull and resistance offered by air.

Exercise 6

Show the following Experiments.

1. Concerning the litmus paper when it is put alternatively in an alkali and an acidic solution.
2. Concerning the mixing up of two solutions - one containing turmeric powder and the other containing washing powder.
3. Concerning the watching of water drops on the outer surface of a glass tumbler when ice cubes are put in it.
4. Concerning the weighing on the same balance of the equal number of fresh green and dry brown leaves of the same tree or plant.
5. Concerning the weighing of a handful of grains before and after being parched on a red hot sheet of iron such as a griddle.

DESCRIBING PEOPLE

Example

You saw a young woman picking an old man's pocket in a bus. But she at once got down from the moving bus and disappeared in the lanes in a crowded area. Give the woman's Description to make the matter easy for the police.

Describing People

The woman was middle aged. She was thin and short-statured.She had a dark complexion. She was wearing no jewellery. She had a black red mole on the left cheek. She had an oval face and a snub nose. Her hair was black and thick. She had a long pig-tail. She was wearing a blue jeans and white top. I couldn't notice her shoes.

Exercise 7

Describe in about 60 words how each of the following looks to you. Give physical appearance and dress only.

1. Your Grandmother
2. Your Best Friend
3. Your Younger Sister
4. Your Maid-servant
5. Your School Peon
6. Your Neighbour
7. Your Favourite Cricketer
8. Your Favourite Actor/Actress

GIVING DIRECTIONS

Examples

Your friend is away to the States. His mother phones you to arrange some plumber as she has some plumbing problem in her house. Give Proper Directions to the plumber to enable him to reach your friend's house.

Directions

We are at present at the Royal Road. Go straight on this road towards the Railway Station. There is a Queen's Street in the Green Park area. Take the first turn on the left to enter the King Street. Study the house numbers. Ring the doorbell at house No.735. A dark complexioned young maid servant or a middle aged woman with an impressive personality will open the door. Ask her if that is Mr David's house. If so, tell her the job and name me, that is, Robert, for having sent you for the purpose.

Exercise 8

1. You are in need of a study table. You approach a carpenter. Explain to him your need giving Directions about the kind of material he should use and when and where he should deliver to you the furnished product.
2. Give Directions to your younger brother who is to attend a birthday party how he should behave there.

DESCRIBING PLACES

Examples

Describe the city you live in, in about 100 words.

I live in Delhi. It is the Capital of India. It is an ancient city. It has several ancient monuments and historical and other places of interest such as the Red Fort, the Qutub Minar, the India Gate, the Parliament House, the Connaught Place, the President House, the Lotus Temple, the Buddha Garden, etc. It is a city of museums, art galleries, parks, universities and libraries. It has a good transport system. Now, the Delhi Metro Railway has also started working over some parts of it. The sacred river, Yamuna, flows through it. With all its hustle and bustle and problems, I love this city very much.

Exercise 9

1. Describe your country in about 100 words.
2. Describe your home in about 100 words.
3. Describe the airport in about 100 words.
4. Describe your study room in about 100 words.
5. Describe your class-room in about 100 words.
6. Describe your city bus stand in about 100 words.
7. Describe your city railway station in about 100 words.

NAMING IMPORTANT PARTS OF OBJECTS

Examples

Name ten important parts of a bicycle.

1. Chassis
2. Saddle
3. Handle
4. Rims
5. Tyres
6. Tubes
7. Chain
8. Pedals
9. Brakes
10. Bell

Exercise 10

1. Name the important parts of a car.
2. Name the important parts of a scooter.
3. Name some important parts of a ship.
4. Name some important parts of a Computer.
5. Name some important parts of a Refrigerator.

THE MAKING OF THINGS

Examples

How is a house made? Mention important processes only.

First clay is dug out. Then water is mixed with it to make a muddy dough. Then this dough is put in dies to make bricks. These clay bricks are heated in kilns to bake them.

Then these bricks are transported to the site where the house is to be built.

The masons prepare a paste of cement, sand and other material which they use to fix bricks in a proper order to make walls. Besides fixing ingredients like cement, etc. steel girders and rods are fixed to build the roof.

Now, doors and windows are fixed except for the frames which have already been fixed in the walls.

Later, internal woodwork, sanitary work, etc. are completed. Besides bricks, marble slabs, stone, etc. are also used by certain people, particularly the members of the affluent society.

Exercise 11

1. Describe briefly how paper is made.
2. Describe briefly how clouds appear in the sky.
3. Describe briefly how steel is made.
4. Describe briefly how a book is made.
5. Describe briefly how diamonds get manufactured naturally.
6. Describe briefly how cloth is made.
7. Explain briefly how the solar eclipse is caused.
8. Explain briefly how the lunar eclipse is caused.

ENRICH YOUR GRAMMAR EIGHT

ANSWERS

Unit 1 (Page 7)

Exercise 1

1 a, a 2. The, the 3. an 4. an
5. The 6. the 7. an, the 8. the
9. the, the 10. a, a/the 11. the, the 12. a, the
13. The, the 14. the 15. a, the

Exercise 2

1. a, the 2. the, an 3. A, the
4. the, a 5. the, the, x 6. The, a, a, the
7. The, the 8. a, a, a, the 9. a, the
10. a, x, a 11. a, a, x, the, x 12. the, the

Unit 2 (Page 13)

Exercise 1

1. anyone 2. Somebody
3. Everyone 4. Nobody
5. someone 6. someone, anyone
7. Nothing 8. No one
9. anyone 10. anything, nothing
11. One 12. Nothing
13. something 14. Everyone
15. nothing 16. Everybody, something
17. somebody/anybody 18. Somebody
19. Nobody 20. Nobody

Unit 3 (Page 15)

Exercise 1

1. Alex is the most outstanding in our class.
2. One of my cousins is in the habit of talking non-stop for hours together. I think he is the most Loquacious person in the world.
3. Henry takes immense pleasure in hooting and whistling. He is the noisiest student in our class.
4. The car Mr. Hood bought yesterday is flashier than yours.
5. Maria beat the curd for a few minutes to make it soft and fluffy.
6. There are all kinds of comforts in his house. So, it is the most luxurious house in the world.
7. Yesterday, a car met with an accident on the highway. All the occupants got injuries but the condition of the driver was the worst.
8. His next plan was even more atrocious than the previous one.
9. Now, the naughty boys thought that it was time for them to take risk. Tomy seemed to be the most audacious among them all.
10. He was brought up in the gloomiest place in the world.

Exercise 2

1. (b) Very few medicines are as bitter as quinine.
   (c) Quinine is one of the most bitter medicines.
2 (b) Miley is not more industrious than Lolita.
3 (b) Very few trains in India are as fast as Rajdhani Express.
   (c) The Rajdhani Express is faster than most other trains in India.
4. (b) No other singer in the world is as delightful as he.
   (c) He is more delightful than any other singer in the world.
5. (b) This place is more horrifying than any other in the world.
   (c) This is the most horrifying place in the world.
6. (b) No other bird has as iridescent feathers as this one has.
   (c) This bird has more iridescent feathers than any other bird.
7. (b) I have got a purse which is finer than most other purses in the world.
   (c) Very few purses in the world are as fine as I have got.
8. (b) The Taj Mahal is more beautiful than most of the monuments in the world.
   (c) The Taj Mahal is one of the most beautiful monuments in the world.
9. (b) Very few trains in the world are as long as this.
   (c) This train is longer than most of the trains in the world.
10. (b) No other hotel in India is as expensive as this.
   (c) This hotel is more expensive than any other hotel in India.

Unit 4 (Page 20)

Exercise 1

1. Many 2. much 3. many
4. many 5. much, many 6. Many
7. much, many 8. Many 9. many
10. much 11. Many 12. many, much
13. much, many 14. many, much 15. many, much
16. much 17. much 18. much

Exercise 2

1. a few 2. little 3. little
4. Few 5. little 6. a little
7. little 8. a few 9. a little
10. A little 11. little 12. few

Exercise 3

1. The few 2. The little 3. The little
4. The few 5. the little 6. The little
7. The few 8. The few

Exercise 4

1. fewer 2. fewer 3. less
4. fewer 5. fewer 6. fewer
7. less 8. less 9. fewer
10. less

Exercise 5

1. Every 2. either 3. Each 4. every
5. Neither 6. either 7. Each 8. every
9. each 10. Either 11. either 12. each
13. Neither 14. Every 15. Every

Exercise 6

1. any, some 2. some, any 3. some
4. some, any 5. some 6. any, some
7. any, some 8. any, some 9. some, any
10. any, some 11. any, some 12. any, some
13. some, any 14. some, some 15. any, some
16. some, any 17. any, some 18. any, some
19. some, any 20. some, any

Unit 5 (Page 27)

Exercise 1

1. drinks, is drinking
2. is painting, does
3. plays, is playing
4. are you doing, want
5. is going, hope
6. rains
7. love
8. goes, is going
9. smokes, is smoking
10. are asked
11. speaks, is speaking
12. likes, is going
13. are, seems
14. does, is losing
15. plays, is playing
16. come
17. is
18. is trying
19. tease
20. works, is going

Exercise 2

1. lived
2. visited
3. wore, was wearing
4. met, was caring
5. blew, was, was blowing
6. flew
7. danced, sang
8. transported
9. put, moved, flung
10. was looking for
11. was, began
12. went, was listening to, was
13. was, showed, came
14. played, was playing
15. wanted, showed, kept
16. was, began, was left
17. met, was
18. caused, regained, looked
19. saw, was talking
20. turned, started, were brushing

Exercise 3

1. Have, been
2. skidded
3. went
4. has just come
5. has decided
6. have finished
7. I have not seen, met
8. have had
9. has worked
10. watched, have
11. has, launched
12. knew
13. has made
14. saw
15 have finished
16. have, finished
17. was, had, has earned
18. have already appeared
19. have, thought of
20. seemed, has gone

Exercise 4

1. had rubbed, went
2. did not make, decided
3. reached, had already been
4. saw, impressed
5. had died, reached
6. had, been informed, did not pay, had said
7. got, had come
8. promised, came, had, made
9. had taken off, reached
10. broke into, woke up, had, gone
11. had switched off
12. had, taken, called on
13. told, had not committed
14. had tunnelled, went, found, had been

Exercise 5

1. has been operating
2. had been living
3. had been drawing
4. had been learning

Exercise 6

1. will have been singing, arrive
2. will have been painting
3. will have been washing, reach
4. will be telling, reach
5. will have been decorating
6. will, have received
7. will not go, come
8. will not leave, am
9. prepares, will submit
10. will be, work, stand
11. will have been knitting
12. will have been learning
13. will get, lose
14. will, get, are

Unit 6 (Page 38)

Exercise 1

1. were
2. had read
3. had been
4. had
5. put on
6. Were
7. Would
8. Had
9. would have got
10. had been
11. had not anchored
12. had brushed
13. Had I placed
14. would have died
15. were
16. Had he not tasted
17. were
18. had
19. had been
20. would have attended

Exercise 2

2. If I had been a doctor, I would not have charged any fee from the poor.
3. If I had flown an aeroplane, I would have been more alert.
4. If I had had more money, I would have bought a big car.
5. If my brother had got an exotic pen, he would have written fast and neatly.
6. If my aunt had baked a cake, she would have beaten the egg and butter properly.
7. If I had been the Prime Minister, I would have not allowed my neighbours to make nuclear weapons.
8. If I had been a dress designer, I would have stitched only the children's dresses.
9. If you had played the piano, you would have enthralled the audience.
10. If you had smoked too much you would have fallen a victim to some dangerous disease.

Unit 7 (Page 41)

Exercise 1

1. Can, can't, can
2. may
3. used to
4. needn't, can
5. dare
6. cannot, could
7. shall
8. should not, will
9. Would
10. Would
11. ought
12. may
13. will not
14. must
15. May
16. will
17. will
18. Could, can
19. used to be, would
20. can, can't, ought to, can
21. needn't
22. had to
23. Shall/Should
24. Will
25. Can

Exercise 2

1. needn't
2. Should
3. would
4. May
5. Could
6. dared not

7. May	8. ought to
9. used to	10. shall
11. had to	12. shall not
13. must, will	14. can, could
15. would	

Unit 8 (Page 51)

Exercise 1

1. Neither war nor calmness has given relief to his jumpy nerves.
2. ✓
3. Colin or his friends are going to visit the dog shop.
4. Jack or his mother is being approached by the company for finance.
5. Neither David nor his relatives were present at the ball.
6. Either her friends or Nadia is being called to start the election campaign.
7. Neither Peter nor his brother takes interest in games.
8. Rosy or Nina is to be selected for dance competition.
9. Either aunt Mary or Nina has baked this delicious cake.
10. Tanks or Jumbo Jet is being sent to the border.

Exercise 2

1. Brick and stone is used to build houses.
2. ✓
3. The committee were divided on the decision of arrangement of funds.
4. The black and white birds fly in the sky.
5. The fat hen and the thin dog have already lost the race.
6. ✓
7. ✓
8. The furniture is made up of wood and metal.
9. He walks as if he were a king.
10. Lily talks as though she were a queen.

Exercise 3

1. Tina along with her sisters was cordially invited on the. auspicious of the marriage of Mrs. Mary's daughter.
2. ✓
3. The boys as well as their uncle have been asked to assist the police in their investigation of the case.
4. The carpenter along with other apprentices has completed the wooden work in time.
5. ✓
6. The chickens as well as their mother have been put to feeding grains.

Unit 9 (Page 56)

Exercise 1

1. Rosy and Dolly are going to America tonight.
2. Danny or Henry will not be sanctioned leave for a week. /Neither Danny nor Henry will be sanctioned leave for a week.
3. Clip the hedges of my lawn or leave the place.
4. The Newspaper was full of glaring errors yet David understood it all.
5. Put manure to the plants soon or they may wither.
6. Our landlord is rich but unkind.
7. John knows dancing and singing well.
8. It was an old ramshackle but I managed to drive it to the garage.
9. My watch is out of order but the watch of my sister is working properly.
10. The clouds of smoke were emerging from the chimney and were slowly engulfing the entire atmosphere over the area.

Exercise 2

1. If	2. As soon as	3. when
4. lest	5. If	6. in case
7. since	8. before	9. after
10. when	11. until	12. but
13. unless	14. provided that	

Exercise 3

1. The arrow pierced his heart while he was sitting in his chair.
2. Hands off this yummy cake or you'll be scolded by Mary.
3. The cobbler demanded a box of dubbin since he wanted to soften leather.
4. The sun rises and its alpenglow spreads over the distant mountains.
5. She could not set aside any money for future because she was extravagant.
6. He was asked to choose from a great many old articles when he took a highly burnished steel cap which belonged to her grandpapa Colonel Wood.
7. You won't indulge in gossip because you have to finish your homework before sunset.
8. Her knowledge put the adroit workforce of the company to shame, so she was immediately offered a high post in the company.
9. He realized that he was lacking in the necessary academic qualities to be taken as a university scholar as he started taking interest in film industry.
10. She can't go abroad until she has to get her visa from MEA.
11. The roads of Singapore were cleared of all traffic as the caravans of Ambassador from almost all corners of the world were about to pass.

Unit 10 (Page 62)

Exercise 1

1. at	2. at, in	3. above	4. over
5. at, in, on	6. by/at	7. in/into	8. In front of
9. under, on	10. on, by	11. across	12. along
13. through	14. over, in/into	15. into	

Exercise 2

1. During	2. throughout	3. from
4. at/by	5. for	6. at, on, in, in
7. throughout, before	8. on	9. till
10. By	11. On	12. for
13. from	14. on, at	15. before

Exercise 3

1. of	2. with	3. with, from
4. in, for	5. with, for	6. of
7. with, with	8. with, for	9. with, in, by
10. by	11. with	12. of
13. to, with	14. by	15. by

Exercise 4

1. but	2. of	3. In spite
4. by	5. with, with	6. at
7. but	8. by	9. of
10. above	11. by, in	12. with, of
13. In spite of, at	14. about	15. by

Exercise 5

1. (c)	2. (a)	3. (a)	4. (b)	5. (c)
6. (a)	7. (a)	8. (b)	9. (a)	10. (c)
11. (c)	12. (a)	13. (a)	14. (b)	15. (c)
16. (a)	17. (a)	18. (b)	19. (a)	20. (b)

21.	(c)	22.	(b)	23.	(b)	24.	(a)	25.	(a)
26.	(c)	27.	(a)	28.	(b)	29.	(a)	30.	(a)

Exercise 6

1.	into	2.	of	3.	of
4.	in, with, for, with	5.	against, with	6.	on
7.	from	8.	of	9.	to
10.	with	11.	at	12.	of
13.	of	14.	to, for	15.	with
16.	to	17.	in, at	18.	over
19.	of	20.	of	21.	to
22.	for, of, to, of	23.	for	24.	to, to
25.	at, of	26.	of, in	27.	to, for
28.	to, into	29.	with, of	30.	at
31.	with	32.	at/on	33.	from
34.	to	35.	to	36.	at
37.	for	38.	at, on	39.	for, on
40.	to	41.	in	42.	at
43.	on	44.	of	45.	at, for, to
46.	across	47.	after	48.	of
49.	at	50.	to	51.	with
52.	with	53.	from, in	54.	off, on
55.	at	56.	of, to	57.	to, for
58.	to/with	59.	of, about, from	60.	with, away
61.	At, to	62.	about	63.	of
64.	at	65.	from, to	66.	with
67.	off	68.	of	69.	to
70.	to	71.	into	72.	for
73.	down	74.	into	75.	in
76.	for	77.	in	78.	to
79.	to	80.	against/into		

Unit 11 (Page 75)

Exercise 1

1. The toothpaste was squeezed with all her strength by Karina.
2. Wool was spun into the yarn by some worker.
3. This case will be reviewed by my uncle.
4. The lid was removed over the bowl by the chef.
5. The river was rowed across by her alone.
6. All the things on the shelf have been put in a good manner by Martin.
7. A new scheme to control information had already been proposed by the defence minister.
8. None is waited for by time and tide.
9. His dresses are usually dumped on the bed by Jack.
10. The sledge will have been dragged by the snow dogs.
11. Comics and detective novels are being read by the students.
12. Some grains and bananas were being looked for by the monkey.

Exercise 2

1. What was being done by the lion in the jungle?
2. Why is the matter being taken so seriously by you?
3. Who is wanted to be seen by you?
4. Where has the aircraft been seen by you?
5. By whom were these bones buried under the soil?
6. How was the mountain crossed so easily by her?
7. Why will Mr. John be appointed as the manager by you?
8. By whom were the gangsters nabbed?
9. What had been purchased from New Zealand by him during his trip?
10. By whom will the cat be belled?

Exercise 3

1. You are advised to work hard.
2. Has your examination been fared well in by you?
3. Are the pictures being coloured by the boys?
4. You are requested to sit down.
5. You are ordered to post this letter at once.
6. It is wished that you should live long.
7. It is prayed that you may stand first in the class.
8. Sugar is sweet when it is tasted.
9. Silk is soft when it is touched.
10. The beggar was laughed at by the boys.
11. Te door was knocked on by Jack.
12. Were any imprints of her paws left by the lioness?
13. Was the piece of cake being looked at merrily by the mice?
14. It is suggested that we should have some snacks and tea.
15. Could your pen be used by me?
16. It is prayed that you may be prosperous.
17. He was impressed a lot by her austere simplicity.
18. You are commanded not to move./You are forbidden to move.
19. He is known to me very well.
20. I was annoyed at his behaviour.

Exercise 4

1. Tina turned on the radio.
2. It is time to open the shop.
3. Harry bangs shut the book.
4. They say that some plants are dwarf-trees.
5. The driver is driving the truck at a terrific speed.
6. After the blast, the sea authorities were searching the ship.
7. Did the fairy swish the wand in the air?
8. Is a trainee pilot flying the aeroplane?
9. A spider has trapped the fly into its web.
10. The gardener had given round ends to the hedges.
11. A multinational company is selling the shampoo blended with henna.
12. Has the warrior flown a burnished arrow over the battlefield as a warning?
13. Don't touch my books.
14. Let us sit under the tree.
15. Please help me solve this sum.
16. Should we send a message to him?
17. Wax is greasy to touch.
18. I know him.
19. Why has the government not allowed this company to operate in Singapore?
20. Were the farmers broadcasting the dry seeds in the fields?

Unit 12 (Page 86)

Exercise 1

1. Harry says that it rains heavily on the hill-side.
2. Tina will say that her mother is cutting vegetables and fruits. They are expecting guests today.
3. Jack will tell Peter that he has seen this boy somewhere before.
4. Mary tells Lily that a carpenter is expert in driving the nails properly in wood.
5. James tells Marry that the prince came out with a burnished sword.
6. Maya will say that you (or I) must apply for this post.
7. Kelly tells Simmy that the gangsters bound her hand and foot.
8. Robert will tell Jacob that he wants to buy these lightweight sunglasses.

Exercise 2

1. Sam says Victor, "The trees in the forest are being cut by the smugglers and are being sold to the foreigners at high prices."

2. Barry says, "My uncle, being a member of the crew, often keeps sailing through the seas."
3. Tony says, "The golden rays of the sun fall on the fluffy clouds in a beautiful pattern."
4. David says to James, "I have no time to see my own weaknesses."
5. Sophia says to Annie, "I will shoot an angular goal in the final match and will become victorious."
6. The child says to his mother, "I have drunk half a glass of milk and the rest of the milk I will take after playing with my friend."
7. The boy says to his friends, "The elephant gave a yank to the berry tree and soon after, it snapped in two."
8. The girl says to her aunt, "Whenever I tried to walk over the marble floor, I had a fall for its being so slippery."
9. He says, "My brother will explore the forest on foot."
10. The servant says to the master, "I could not work properly yesterday because I was not feeling well."

Exercise 3

1. Harry told Parker that Daisy had just qualified as a doctor.
2. Tina told Ruby that John had been rebuked for making a noise.
3. Miley told Julie that they were getting their house rebuilt.
4. Henry told Robin that the police often recover a large number of stolen articles from the gangs of robbers.
5. Lily told Maya that the manager had recorded her statement.
6. Mr. Gower told his secretary that he was not working on this topic in a proper manner.
7. John told Martin that he was happy that he still held fast to that principle.
8. Max told Alex that he did not know how to make a good job of it.
9. Tony told Paul that it was good if he clamped that plank to the edge of that table.
10. John told Lily that he/she hadn't even finished his/her work yet.

Exercise 4

1. The tailor said to the actor, "A sea green, might gown looks good on you."
2. The girl said to her mother, "I have definitely made up her deficiency in studies now."
3. The private detective said to the police man, "I have seen the thief running but I take him for an innocent man and let him run away."
4. Sam said to John, "The sale of ready-made garments is going to be a lucrative one because some of the foreign companies have shown great interest in the Indian garments."
5. The old man said to us, "A big cache of arms have been seized by the local police."
6. The businessman said to the share holders, "The company has decided to increase the production of nylon fibre and for this it is going to raise funds."
7. The scientist said to the science students, "Ever since the plants have appeared on the earth they have been serving mankind without demur."
8. The boy said, "I have already seen the eruption of the volcano when I was working in a hilly earthquake prone region of the country."
9. The hunter said to the boy, "I haven't even killed a forest animal but I have trapped a few whom I have sold to the master of a circus."
10. The old lady said to the press reporter, "The boat I am sailing in has once capsized all of a sudden."

> **Note :** In a few cases, past indefinite might seem better than present perfect, but in view of academic exercises here, we try to stick to rules to avoid confusion.

Exercise 5

1. Robert told Kelvin that he had crossed the bridge within a few minutes.
2. Shelly told Rosy that the boys had been holding bouquets of flowers while the girls had been giving them instructions.
3. Harry told John that they had already arranged a military band to make the celebrations a memorable event.
4. Lucy told Daizy that her brother's friend had not wished to leave Singapore.
5. Juliet told Rose that the food had not been good and the drinks had not been up to mark either in the party.
6. Jack told Mr. Ford that he had not said anything about the bad arrangement of lighting inside the hall.
7. The officer told the farmers that the previous year heavy rains affected the crops badly.
8. The manager told the head chef that his subordinates had not been cooking good dishes.
9. Peter told Martin that his friends had been drawing a cart when he went to see them.
10. Jane told Mary that her brother had not known how to drive a steamer.

> **Note** : In some cases the use of past indefinite or past continues instead of past perfect and past perfect continuous might seem all right to convey the desired sense but in view of the academic exercises here, we try to stick to rules to avoid confusion.

Exercise 6

1. Julia said to Tina, "I made a heavy purchase at the sales counter in the City Garments yesterday."
2. The fisherman said to me, "Once I was looking for a big catch at sea when giant fish crashes into my boat."
3. The chef said to the waiter, "I have put the kettle on the stove and am now waiting for tea to boil."
4. The soldier said to his friends, "I saw a terrorist crawling out of a hideout."
5. The child said to the teacher, "I have coloured all the pictures with crayons."
6. The nurse said to the patient's friend, "The patient has been allowed to amble about in the lawn for an hour."
7. Lily said to Karina, "I was brushing my hair when a cold gale ruffled it."
8. The hunter said to the boys, "The horseman whipped the horse to gallop."
9. My aunt said to me, "I haven't ever liked the children weeping for chocolates and toffees."
10. The botanist said to the fruitseller, "The apples on the trees are being injected with newly invented drugs to increase their sizes."

Exercise 7

1. Tony told Riya that the big diamond would have been cut by them.
2. Gomes told Simmy that he would not purchase a lidless dustbin.
3. Danny told Max that the cat would be licking her injured paw.
4. Julie told Mary that she would get tangy snacks and other eatables at the school tuck-shop.
5. The mother told the child that he would not keep anything back from her.

6. The coach told the players that just one sip of this tonic will boost up their drooping spirits.
7. The gatekeeper told the boy that he would be informed soon about it.
8. The shopkeeper told the customer that he would not exchange that old chair for a new one.
9. The boy told his friend that the next day his uncle would be given a green signal to go abroad.
10. John told Peter that he wouldn't be allowed to keep all the coins with himself.

Exercise 8

1. My aunt said to my mother, "My son will have learned manners by now."
2. My brother said to my sister, "You will be getting your hair curled when the guests appeared."
3. Henry said to Charles, "I will definitely fight for the rights of the poor people."
4. Tina said to her brother, "I will have definitely completed my thesis by the end of this month."
5. Rosy said to Timmy, "My brother will take part in the Olympics the next year."
6. The student said to the teacher, "I will work hard and win the scholarship."
7. Lolita said to Ruby, "My mother will fall a victim to influenza because she is still strolling in the lawn when the evening has turned so bitterly cold."
8. My uncle said to us, "The cubs will cling together as the night gets colder."
9. The old woman said to the investigator, "I will see the robber through the glass window."
10. The old man said to the optician, "I will not spend much on the glasses because I am not going to be helped by them in any way for my being blind."

Exercise 9

1. Alex advised Martin to work hard.
2. James requested Maya to give him a glass of water.
3. Lily commanded Peter not to move./Lily forbade Peter to move.
4. Adam suggested to Harry that they should have a cup of tea/Adam suggested that Harry and he should have a cup of tea.
5. John offered Mary some snacks.
6. Mendis requested Feroz to listen to him.
7. Mr. Simon suggested to Mr. David that they should have some walk.
8. Tina forbade Rosy to disturb her.
9. Harry requested Lily to wait for him.
10. Max ordered Ford to stop there.

Exercise 10

1. Julie said to her sister, "Learn various arts to succeed in life."
2. John said to his friends, "Let us have a short walk daily."
3. The teacher said to the student, "Stand up on the bench."
4. My friend said to me, "Please buy me a new pen from the main market."
5. The gardener said to the children, "Don't play in the garden."
6. Mr. Hood said to Mr. David, "Have some snacks."
7. My aunt said to me, "Get up with the first ray of sun and take some exercise to keep fresh both body and mind."
8. I said to my friend, "Please bring me some poster, colours and brushes from the nearby shop."
9. My friend, shivering with cold, said, "Let us sit around a roaring fire and have a scalding hot coffee."
10. The police officer said to the prisoner, "Don't do anything wrong in future."

Exercise 11

1. The old man wished that I might live long.
2. The old woman cursed me wishing that I might fail in my mission.
3. The old woman prayed/wished that I might prosper.
4. The girl exclaimed with joy that it was a beautiful snail.
5. The boy exclaimed with joy that crown is very beautiful.
6. The old man wished that I might become rich.
7. The child exclaimed with joy/surprise that the animal was very huge.
8. The girl exclaimed with contempt that, that oil gave a very foul smell.
9. My grandmother prayed/wished that I might get success in my enterprise.
10. My uncle exclaimed with joy/surprise that, that bird was very strange.

Exercise 12

1. The old woman said, "May you be victorious in your venture!"
2. The old man said to the king, "May you lose all your wealth as well as fame!"
3. The child said, "How beautiful the stars look!"
4. The girl said, "Strange! The aeroplane is looking like a bird."
5. The girl said, "How ugly the wild beast is!"
6. The woman said, "Wow! My husband has trimmed down to 70 kg in just two months."
7. The beggar said, "May mankind live in peace!"
8. The old man said, "May man be provided with wisdom!"
9. The child said, "What a beautiful painting it is!"
10. The old woman said to the naughty boy, "May you fail in the examination!"

Exercise 13

1. John asked Tony if he should hire a taxi for him.
2. Robin asked Bobby if he would apply oil to his new motorbike.
3. Paul asked Twinkle if she could drive the car through that muddy street.
4. Daisy asked Lily if she would like to dance with her.
5. Sophia asked Maria if she had decided to emigrate to England.
6. Tina asked Peter if he was ready to help her.
7. Alice asked Lolita if she knew the exact meaning of that word.
8. Henry asked Max if his brother had sailed the boat across the river.
9. Adam asked Peter if his sister was learning martial arts those days.
10. Mr. Paul asked Mr. David if he understood the language of birds.
11. The Lawyer asked the culprit if he had really misappropriated the funds of the trust.
12. The woodcutter asked the god Mercury if he couldn't make the people learn the value of flora and fauna.
13. The boy asked his friend if he didn't get hold of such a simple idea.
14. The girl asked her uncle if the army had set off on the campaign Sarpnash.
15. The teacher asked the student if there were any questions excessively tough.

Exercise 14

1. Lucy said to Jane, "Can you count the snail shells lying on the beach?"
2. Tina said to Sara, "Have you boiled the eggs for the guests?"

3. Juck said to Adam, "Will you affix the stamps to the top of the letters for me?"
4. Dolly said to Rose, "Is your father working as a manager in a five star hotel?"
5. Sunny said to Daizy, "Have you applied for the job of a navy officer?"
6. The shopkeeper said to the customer, "Will you like to see some more exotic pairs of shoes?"
7. The child said to her mother, "Is there some more fresh cheese in the tray?"
8. The old man said to his son, "Can I use your motorbike?"
9. The wife said to her husband, "Will you allow me to purchase some dresses from the sales counter?"
10. The boy said to the shopkeeper, "Can you cut off a length of wire from the coil?"

Exercise 15

1. The customer asked the shopkeeper when he should come again to him for table knives, forks and burnished spoons.
2. The husband demanded of his wife why she was boiling with rage.
3. The conductor demanded of the passenger why he hadn't purchased the ticket.
4. The mother asked the son when he would have finished his homework.
5. Karina asked Joe where he had put his wallet.
6. The mother demanded of the daughter why she didn't do such chores by herself.
7. Nancy asked Ruby how fast the waiter had served them meal.
8. Lily demanded of John why he was apprehensive of the future.
9. The businessman demanded of the sea-men why they had released his vessel into the sea then.
10. The cowboy asked the officer when he should go to the hillside to bring back the cattle.

Exercise 16

1. The child said to his mother, "When should I ask for chocolates and toffees?"
2. The cobbler said to the customer, "Why do you want your boots to be given stitching along the back part?"
3. The officer said to the car driver, "From where have you bought/did you buy that wheel-clamp?"
4. Maria said to Julie, "How have you managed/did you manage to make good your escape?"
5. David said to Robert, "When have you had/did you have a close shave with a tiger?"
6. The officer said to the driver, "What does make you stop the lorry well before the traffic lights?"
7. The teacher said to the student, "Why have you created/did you create a disturbance in the class?"
8. The instructor said to the student, "Why have you not allowed/did you not allow the solution to come to boil when you have been Instructed for that?"
9. The doctor said to the patient, "Who has allowed you to move about on crutches?"
10. The soldier said to the prisoner, "When will you divulge the identity of your companions?"

Unit 13 (Page 108)

Exercise 1

1. made of cotton
2. (big)
3. of different colours
4. of teak wood
5. of gloomy poems
6. (true), (honest)
7. full of antiques
8. (black)
9. (black)
10. (poor), (old), of straw
11. (bad)
12. (rosy), (whole)
13. (cruel), of a rare species
14. (old), (jerky)
15. (colourful), of a big size

Exercise 2

1. Mr. Alex bought a new cycle of green colour while his brother bought a motorbike of an old model.
2. His deed of courage made him a hero among the public in a day.
3. Her books lay scattered over the floor of marble.
4. Lily could not remember where she left her ring of gold.
5. Tears trickled down her cheeks full of dryness.
6. The raindrops dashed against the planks of wood around the field.
7. The paper of buff colour of the book looks full of rust.
8. The lump of copper was beaten out into wires of long sizes.
9. She became a painter winning acclaim as she painted some pictures without a match on the canvas.
10. She could not make much progress in life for being a woman full of insincerity.
11. The boat sailed ahead on the sea surface of blue colour.
12. He played extremely well in the match yet he could not register his first win over the player belonging to Sweden.
13. In spite of his best efforts of the best order he could not win a leading position of the leading rank in his party.
14. Last night a gang of robbers broke into a house in my neighboured.
15. The young boy gave a polish to his shoes looking shabby.

Exercise 3

1. to the exit, (slowly)
2. (wonderfully), out of the fence
3. from this place
4. from there
5. (adversely)
6. (remarkably)
7. (straightway)
8. at the time, in the day, (heavily), on the wooden plank
9. (accurately)
10. on the toe
11. (tightly)
12. at home
13. at an alarming speed
14. at the top of her voice
15. in a neat hand

Exercise 4

1. Mr. Smith was the president of this club at a former time.
2. Before leaving the place Tina informed her friend that she would come in no time.
3. A gull flew away in a swift manner.
4. A horror novel has been launched in the recent time in America.
5. Though Jack could not find his own watch, he accepted another one in a cheerful manner in lieu of it.
6. A tall boy stepped out of the house in a cautious manner.
7. Her mother spoke to her daughter in a soft manner as she wanted to instil in her mind the real value of studies.
8. The old feeble pale man fell down in a heavy manner on the dock of the ship.
9. The burnished arrow came zooming and stuck in the wooden door in a deep manner.
10. He laughed in a mood of anger.
11. The maid handled the crockery in a clumsy manner.
12. Miss Marry talked to her brother in a rude manner.
13. The child lost his eraser at some place near to this place.
14. She knocked on the door in a loud manner.
15. The four troops stepped in the onward direction.

Exercise 5

1. <u>to make fun of others</u>
2. <u>to tease the birds and animals</u>
3. <u>to reach the hall on time</u>
4. <u>to type the letter</u>
5. <u>a brace of pigeons</u>
6. <u>Dancing on the marble floor</u>
7. <u>Cutting grass on a hot summer day</u>
8. <u>To drive on this road slowly</u>
9. <u>to meet me again</u>
10. <u>having stolen my watch</u>
11. <u>to see the brave boys</u>
12. <u>to answer my question</u>
13. <u>To sing loudly</u>
14. <u>going abroad</u>
15. <u>To win the first prize</u>

Unit 14 (Page 114)

Exercise 1

1. <u>dog which had black colour</u>
2. <u>which had a long mane</u>
3. <u>which had a dorsal fin of broad width</u>
4. <u>which had a big trunk</u>
5. <u>which have thick leaves full of thorns</u>
6. <u>which has illustrated pages</u>
7. <u>which was made of a burnished metal</u>
8. <u>which had brown colour</u>
9. <u>who had a strong physique</u>
10. <u>which had blade like leaves</u>

Exercise 2

1. The workers have given a call for strike as soon as the present moment starts.
2. We accepted the deal since we had no hesitation.
3. The truck ran so fast that its speed was terrible.
4. I found a ring when I was at this place.
5. He replied such that his honesty was perfect.
6. She opened the door so that her manner was quick.
7. She is in Russia when you think of the present time.
8. The boy's voice was loud as he cried.
9. The horse was cheerful as it accepted husk of grams.
10. She is expecting guests when it is evening.

Exercise 3

1. She wanted that she should eat oranges.
2. He decided that he should stay at home.
3. The officer ordered that the clerk should leave the room at once.
4. Maria proposed that we should have a cup of tea.
5. The clerk requested that he should be granted leave for two days.
6. I advised that he should work hard.
7. He was allowed that he could/should carry on his business.
8. She was anxious that she should top the list of successful candidates.
9. The teacher ordered that he should bring the file.
10. We decided that we should live in India forever.

Unit 15 (Page 118)

Exercise 1

1. where	2. why	3. when
4. when	5. where	6. why
7. why	8. how	9. when
10. where	11. why	12. where

Exercise 2

2. The reason is still not known to anybody why he loves his sister so much.
3. You should learn the method how these sums can be solved.
4. Canada is the country where apples of good quality are found.
5. Every was surprised/amazed at the way how he managed to save the drowning child.
6. You should try to understand the reason why he beat your dog so mercilessly.
7. Sunday is the day when I go to the beach.
8. The police have learned the tactics how now they can catch the thieves without delay.
9. These are the museums where you can see the pastels and models of skeletons of the dinosaurs there.
10. Nobody knows the reason why Paul does not like his studies.

Unit 16 (Page 120)

Exercise 1

1. who	2. which	3. which
4. that/which	5. such as	6. such as
7. which	8. that	9. which
10. who	11. whose	12. which
13. who	14. who	15. which

Exercise 2

2. I like the plants whose flowers give out a sweet smell.
3. My uncle likes the garden which is ablaze with violet blossoms.
4. Kelly likes the birds which sing melodious songs.
5. The dog which was as strong as tiger, bit at the thief's hand last night.
6. The fisherman wanted to catch the fish which jumped over the surface of water and again came back spinning in the air.
7. The farmer ploughed the fields which were dry and cracked.
8. The student who was making faces at the teacher was punished by the teacher.
9. Tina brushed the hair of her doll which was gifted by Riya's aunt.
10. The cat scratched at the door which was closed.

Exercise 3

1. whichever	2. whoever	3. whoever
4. whatever	5. whoever	6. whoever
7. whoever	8. whatever	9. whatever
10. whoever		

Unit 17 (Page 123)

Exercise 1

1. It was too cold for anyone to go outside.
2. She uselessly tried hard to get at the bunch of grapes.
3. Avogadro was an Italian chemist.
4. Having finished levelling the ground in the lawn Peter went out of the house to see his friends.
5. No one got up in Mr. John's house after the sunrise.
6. He went to see the movie every weekend.
7. Deceived by his rival he decided to leave his country.
8. Being tired he wanted some rest.
9. Having killed some innocent animals the hunter sat down to smoke.
10. Mr. Ford drinks a cup of tea daily in the morning.
11. Shakespeare, a famous dramatist, wrote Macbeth and Othello.

12. Glasgow, a city in scotland, is an important commercial centre.
13. Having broken into the house, the thief stole all the valuables from there.
14. He is too dull to understand his lessons.
15. The book was too heavy for the child to carry it to school.

Exercise 2

1. She is tall but thin.
2. He is good both at sports and studies.
3. Dance with us or you should go out of the hall.
4. Don't go close to that dog or it may bite you in the leg.
5. Neither Harry nor Sheila was ready to purchase the bag.
6. She was tired and sat down under the tree.
7. Mrs. James is slim but active.
8. It was severely cold and I switched on the room-heater.
9. The tree stood bolt upright, yet the boy climbed it.
10. Twinkle can write both German and English correctly.
11. He has attended many periods in the institute to learn spoken English but still he cannot speak English fluently.
12. Don't be in a hurry or/otherwise you may forget to carry some important documents.
13. She can neither sing nor dance well.
14. His mother and sister cook tasty dishes.
15. Timmy daily gets up early in the morning and goes out for a short walk.

Exercise 3

1. The bull which was brought to India could engage even a lion in a fight.
2. This is the station where every train stops for five minutes.
3. This is the boat which has never capsized during the past five years.
4. This is the boy whose casual attitude towards studies is going to stall his success in life.
5. The boy from whom I have borrowed five hundred dollars is good.
6. This is the road which leads to Nairobi.
7. This the girl whose mother is an army officer.
8. The boa which/that I saw in the forest of America was very strong.
9. Can you tell me the reason why you are not working properly?
10. The king who was not wearing an armour, was killed.

Exercise 4

1. I want to know whether you have a gum.
2. She told me that her brother had been working in a factory since 1999.
3. I want to know why you smoke.
4. He asked me who knocked on the door.
5. He explained to me why he did not want to leave his own house at any cost.
6. My teacher brought home to the students that the earth revolves round the sun.
7. My uncle told me that the jewellery box was not carried by the thief.
8. We all know that John shot the winning goal.
9. Can anybody tell me why he was not selected in school cricket eleven.
10. Maya tells her mother that she has finished her homework.

Exercise 5

1. He could not climb Mount Everest because he was afraid of high places.
2. Wait here until I come back.
3. You cannot get success unless you work hard.
4. Though he walked fast, he could not reach the airport on time.
5. As soon as the thief saw the policeman, he ran away.
6. He worked till late at night so that he could stand first in the class.
7. She could not win the first prize though she made an impressive speech.
8. The python remained coiled round his neck until it was killed later by the people.
9. She typed fast so that she could complete the work before sunset.
10. He could not attend the meeting because he had to fly to New Zealand.

Unit 18 (Page 134)

Exercise 1

1. Although the novel was full of errors, the reader managed to understand the actual story
2. He got success because he tried hard
3. If you do not stop teasing the birds, you will be punished
4. You cannot be allowed to meet the Prime Minister unless you give me your camera
5. He won the first prize because he wrote a very good essay
6. The child cut the mushrooms into small pieces with the knife which was sharp
7. Although he wept bitterly, his mother did not buy him a kite
8. Although the lion roared loudly, it could not terrorize the child
9. If you do not stop disturbing me, you will be thrown out of the room
10. She was liked by all because she sang sweetly

Exercise 2

1. You cannot get good marks in the examination without listening to your teacher.
2. In spite of being weak in mathematics, he managed to get pass marks.
3. Being extremely busy, he could not attend the guests.
4. Having got up late that morning, he could not attend the meeting.
5. In order to get relief from the scorching heat of the sun, he dived into the tank.
6. The girl plucked the flowers in order to make a bouquet to present it to her teacher.
7. In case of his putting on a new dress, he will be selected for the new film.
8. Despite the heavy rain, he could make it to his house.
9. His friend's finishing his dinner so fast amazed John.
10. Being not aware about his financial position, she could not help him.

Exercise 3

1. In spite of the train being fast, he got down from it quickly.
2. In case of your talking, you may be punished.
3. In spite of working hard, she could not clear the examination.
4. Besides breaking the chair, Robin made much noise.
5. In case of your [illegible] working hard, you are going to lose your five dollars.
6. In spite of running fast, he could not win the race.
7. In spite of being fat, he was very active.
8. You must play well to escape losing the match.
9. Don't laugh to escape being thrown out of these premises.
10. Having cooked the dish, she went into the drawing-room.

Exercise 4

1. This wild beast is very ferocious.
2. Weather is very lovely today.
3. You are a big fool.
4. This is a very big house./This house is very big.
5. This news is very bad.
6. It is very cold.
7. This is a very delicious apple./This apple is very delicious.
8. His head bleeds very badly.
9. It is a very wonderful bird.
10. This dress is very beautiful.

Exercise 5

1. O that I had wings!
2. Alas! Jack is dead.
3. What a beautiful animal this is!
4. What a cheat you are!
5. How well he dances!
6. O that I were rich!
7. How beautiful the rainbow is!
8. How big the blue whale is!
9. What an intelligent girl she is!
10. What a calm place this is!

Unit 19 (Page 141)

Exercise 1

1. They thought him to be a gentleman.
2. I wonder to think how Tina look like in these clothes.
3. He worked hard to earn one million dollars by the end of the year.
4. John was the first boy to enter the hall.
5. He is said to know about future.
6. She sighs to become a play-back singer.
7. I'm glad to know about your having/that you have set up a new office in the heart of the city.
8. We do not expect ever to lose the match.
9. She trembled to see a snake close to her.
10. She was delighted to learn of her father's improved health.

Exercise 2

1. She is clever enough to overcome the obstacle.
2. He is too short to touch the ceiling.
3. Julie is rich enough to buy a new house.
4. This book is too tough for a child to understand.
5. He was too strong enough to give good fight to his rival.
6. She is too weak to walk or sit properly.
7. Sam is not talented enough to be an actor.
8. The monkey was not big enough to climb to the top of the tree.
9. The explosion was too powerful to bring about a great damage to the towering building.
10. This book is not too small for anyone to read it in one sitting.
11. This room is spacious enough for all these boxes to be put in it.
12. The box was too heavy for the boy to carry it to the room.
13. Mary was too busy to get time to sew your shirt.
14. It was too cold outside for me to go anywhere.
15. The weather was pleasant enough for us to go for a picnic.

Unit 20 (Page 144)

Exercise 1

1. I listened to the music coming from the next room.
2. Going to school on the empty road, he heard a strange voice behind his head.
3. I saw the cat, grooming itself.
4. While swimming through the ford, I saw a starfish being carried away by the gigantic water current.
5. I could see the flag, waving in the fast blowing wind.
6. Look at the moon shining calmly.
7. I could hear the old man, crying for help.
8. The child, ascending the stairs with bounding steps, rolled down the stairs.
9. Taking out their guns, the warriors started running towards the border.
10. While looking towards the door, she saw her father entering.
11. She smelt the cake, burning.
12. Sitting under the tree, the old man was mumbling away to himself.
13. While sweeping the floor, the maid found a five-cent coin.
14. They watched the train running at a terrible speed.
15. I can see the boy dancing merrily.

Exercise 2

1. Deceived by his friends, he decided to leave the town.
2. Rejected by all, he decided not to talk to anybody in future.
3. Terrified by the zooming sound of the landing aeroplane, the dog began to run about.
4. Condemned by all, the prince decided to apologise to the people.
5. Beaten by the army, the guerrillas decided to skulk in the hideouts in the alpine ravines.
6. Amazed at the beauty of the wild animal, he decided to have a snap of it.
7. Got hit against the wall in the dark, the boy went unconscious.
8. Situated on the highway, the motel is a big resting place for motorists.
9. Thrown with great force, the stone struck the thief on the head.
10. Driven aside the road by the strong wind, the dry leaves began to heap up.

Exercise 3

1. Having made the dough, she was ready to bake a big cake.
2. Having broken the glass, the boy went out of the house to play.
3. Having applied a dash of lipstick on her lips, the girl looked at her reflection in the mirror.
4. Having attended the meeting, the officer went to Tokyo later.
5. Having broken into the house, the burglar looted whatever he was able to carry (with himself).
6. Having applied the brakes suddenly, the driver got down the lorry.
7. Having feasted on a swarm of mosquitoes, the lizard went back into the hole.
8. Having washed the clothes, she went into the kitchen.
9. Having cut the paper into small pieces, the child put the scissors back on the shelf.
10. Having plucked the flowers, the boy scurried out of the garden.

Unit 25 (Page 177)

Exercise 1

1. Rita,
   Your classmate Tina told me that there will be no fancy dress competition tomorrow.
   Johnny

Exercise 2

1. Lily,
   Your classmate Annie told me that she has found out your lost ring. She'll come to give it to you tomorrow in the morning.
   Diana

Exercise 3

1. John,
   Your friend Peter told me that his brother has come from America. He has brought a few gifts for you. You should go to Peter's and collect your gifts.
   James

Exercise 4

1. Roma,
   Your classmate Dolly told me that there is going to be a special practical class of biology today at 5 p.m. You must not miss it.
   Lily

Exercise 5

1 Mary
  Your classmate Tom asked me to tell you that tomorrow you should bring his chemistry book that you borrowed from him a few days ago.
  John

Unit 26 (Page 187)

Exercise 1

A

1. Mr. Hood was a well-known connoisseur of food, and was hailed as a "Master Gourmet."
2. A waffle is a crisp flat cake with a pattern of squares over it. It is eaten with sweet sauce.
3. The Author did not eat anything in the party because he was puzzled to see the exotic dishes and was unable to decide properly what to start with.
4. A swiss roll is a kind of cake containing jam. Whereas a Swiss roll is sweet, a bread roll is a saltish dish.
5. a) Waffle b) Croissant c) Strawberry gateau d) Swiss Roll e) Cheese baguettes

B

1. Danish pastries were tasty and cheese baguettes were good too.
2. Apple pies were tasty and jam doughnut was good too.
3. Fairy cake was tasty and waffles were good too.
4. Wedding cake was tasty and sponge cake was good too.
5. Cheese and tomato roll was tasty and croissant was good too.

C

1. Mary is a connoisseur of music and can easily tell about different kinds of music.
2. I have made up my mind to do degree in fashion designing
3. A friend in need is a friend indeed.
4. As the patient was in a critical condition, a doctor had to be called in.
5. Mr. Hood wetted his dry lips with a quick sweep of his tongue.
6. Icing has given a charming shape to the cake.
7. I am fond of crispy things more than soft eatables.
8. The sight of the tray of cheese baguettes made my mouth water.
9. At functions guests prefer tasty dishes to empty decorations.
10. Please catch hold of a bowl of pudding before it is finished by the hungry guests.

D

1. ✓	2. ✗	3. ✗	4. ✓
5. ✗	6. ✗	7. ✓	

Exercise 2

A

1. The nature-lover belonged to a particular brand who took pleasure in horrible things.
2. The nature-lover was passing by a house engulfed by fire. It gave him a lot of pleasure when he looked at the tongue like flames of fire, blazing the surroundings with a dazzling light. Outside the house there were people with gloomy faces and tearful eyes. He was so much impressed that he took out his camera and began to shoot.
3. The fizzling sound was that of the burning furniture of the house. It gave him the never-ending pleasure.
4. A number of people tried to console the nature-lover because he was crying and pulling his hair and they thought that he was doing so because he had real sympathy with those who had suffered.

B

1. Fruits were stale and vegetables were bad either.
2. Jam was infested with fungus and pastries were stale either.
3. Ice-cream was stale and drinks were insipid either.
4. Coffee was cold and snacks were unpalatable either.
5. Biscuits were broken and cookies were tasteless either.

C

1. (a) 2. (a) 3. (a) 4. (a) 5. (b) 6. (a)

D

1. (b) 2. (a) 3. (a) 4. (b) 5. (c)

Exercise 3

A

1. The financial condition of small peasants in our country is very bad as they are mostly under heavy debt.
2. A small farmer has a small holding. He is often under heavy debt, which he is unable to pay back. He is illiterate and consequently unable to handle the situation. He has to spend money on the marriage of his daughter and get his addicted son educated. Sometimes he himself falls a victim to some bad habits like drinking and drug-taking. He cannot take advantage of free water and electricity because he has no tubewell of his own and has to buy water from some big farmer.
3. Besides giving free water and electricity, the government should provide tubewells to small farmers at its own cost. Arrangements for free education to small farmers children should be made by the government.
4. A small farmer has to take loans in a big way often to get his daughter married or to get his addicted son educated.

B

1. He has suffered a heavy loss in business, still, he is continuing it.
2. The government provides free water and electricity to farmers in India.
3. Some farmers incur heavy loans.
4. The financial condition of small farmers is miserable.
5. The farmers have to sell their produce in markets.
6. Small farmers often wallow in poverty.

7. More and more people are getting addicted to drugs these days.
8. A marginal farmer has to live in abject poverty.
9. You must avail yourself of this opportunity.
10. An illiterate person has no place in the modern world.

C
1. A farmer's job is to produce food stuffs for people.
2. Usually small farmers are illiterate and addicted to drinks and drugs.
3. The farmer with a small piece of land has to face a number of difficulties such as unpayable debts, inability to take advantage of free water and electricity.
4. Some of the factors that are making the small farmers poorer and poorer are unpayable debts, marriage and education of children, addiction to drinking or drugs etc.
5. The government is also trying to uplift the small farmers by providing them with low interest loans, free water and electricity, etc.

D
2. The small farmers are mostly <u>creditors</u>.
3. Being <u>literate</u>, they are <u>able</u> to handle the situation.
4. The government supplies them electricity at a <u>higher</u> rate.
5. A <u>big</u> farmer is forced by circumstances to go for loans.

E

1. (germany)	2. (valiant)	3. (elite)	4. (bazaar)
5. (broad)	6. (wasp)	7. (conditional)	8. (vision)

Exercise 4

1. A newspaper is the voice of man. Newspapers provide us with news and views of experts in various fields. Through them we keep in touch with current affairs and know about our country's economic condition.
2. Through the newspaper even a common man can rebuke the government or give his views that may be different from those of the government.
3. Matrimonial columns, Advertisements columns, columns for women, children and old people besides information about sports, politics, stock market, science, history etc.
4. We cannot do without a newspaper because reading a newspaper early in the morning has become our habit.

B.

1. scold	2. happened	3. information
4. written	5. perfection	

C.

1. displeased	2. decaying	3. same
4. untrue	5. multiply	

D.
1. Through newspaper we get knowledge about the fluctuating economic condition of our country.
2. Newspapers also keep us in touch with the current affairs.
3. A newspaper works as a bridge between higher authorities and common people.
4. Through newspapers even a common man can express his views on policies of the government.
5. A newspaper is the voice of people.

Exercise 5

A.
1. A healthy man can do a lot of work which an unhealthy, though wealthy one cannot. A healthy man is always self-dependent. A wealthy but ailing one may or may not be. A healthy man can do a lot for his country, but a wealthy being an ailing one cannot as most of his time is spent in managing cure for his diseases.
2. Health brings wealth. If you are healthy, you can work hard and earn a lot. Thus, health can be a source of wealth even for a poor man. A man who is not healthy cannot do much physical or mental work. He also has to spend a lot of time in managing his diseases. Thus, he loses a major chunk of precious time in life. Hence, it is of paramount importance for us to maintain good health, not only for enjoyment of life but also for earning wealth, which itself is necessary for his enjoyment.
3. I can suggest the following ways to keep healthy:-
   (a) Get up early in the morning and go out for a walk.
   (b) Take regularly some light exercise.
   (c) Take fresh simple diet.
   (d) Avoid fat, salt and sugar-laden foods.
   (e) Avoid fried as well as junk foods.
   (f) Take a lot of water.
   (g) Never over eat.
   (h) Keep yourself free from tension.
   (i) Work hard to earn more but never exert beyond your physical or mental capacity.
   (j) Develop the habit of thinking positively.
   (k) Never allow evil thoughts to enter your mind.

B.

1. c	2. c	3. a	4. c	5. c

C.

1. sick, ailing	2. sound	3. rich	4. engrossed	5. fetch

D.

1. infect	2. poor	3. worse	4. repulsion	5. small

E.
1. Health is wealth.
2. A healthy man is always happy.
3. A nation will prefer a healthy person to a wealthy one because the former has a lot of physical as well as mental capacity to do something for it.
4. Achieving joy in different fields is easy for a healthy person because he has the required strength, will and Inclination, to work for it and win it.